volume 1: to 1865

Promises to Keep

A portrayal of nonwhites in the United States

Bruce A. Glasrud and Alan M. Smith

California State College at Hayward

Rand McNally & Company Chicago

Second Printing, 1972

Promises to Keep

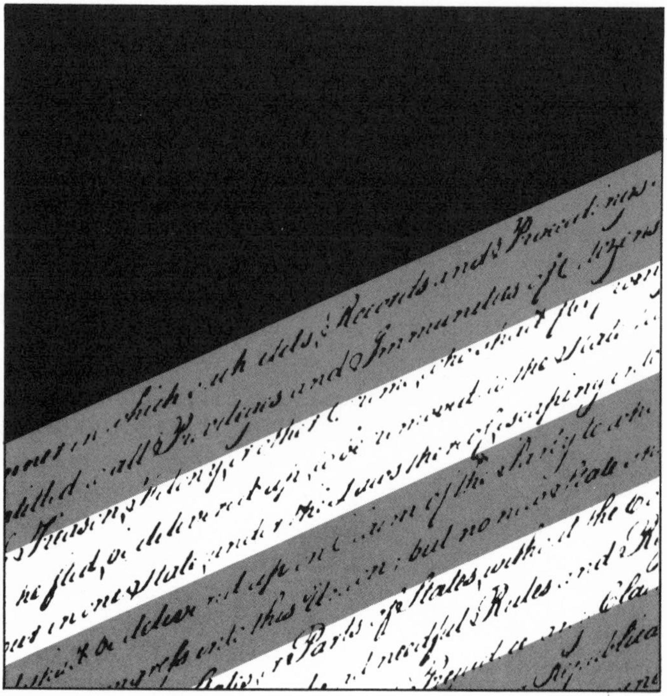

Preface

This book is designed to provide a series of collateral readings on the history of nonwhite Americans for students of United States history. Although many standard American history textbooks have recently been revised to correct their almost total neglect of these minorities, the result in most cases is a token appearance of dark-skinned characters in what is essentially a white man's story. The obvious need for materials treating nonwhites in American history courses has been met by a number of readers on specific minority groups. This book presents readings dealing with the history of all the major nonwhite groups that have played a part in the development of America.

The term "nonwhite" is difficult to define. In this work, we have included articles about Americans who have viewed themselves, or who have been viewed by the white majority, as distinct and different because of their skin color. The groups included—the Indians, blacks, Mexican-Americans, Chinese-Americans, Japanese-Americans, Filipino-Americans, and Puerto Ricans—differ greatly in their roles and experiences in American history, but all have encountered prejudice and difficulties on account of their skin color.

The articles which compose this volume are arranged under six chronological headings covering American history from the founding of Jamestown to the present. In each historical period there is an article concerning the nonwhite groups in American society at that particular time; there are also several articles which cover the relationships among nonwhite groups. The articles are the work of scholarly students of America, most of them historians, writing during the past thirty years. The authors vary in their focuses and points of view, but all are concerned with the interaction between the nonwhite minorities and the white majority in the United States. In most cases, the articles have been edited for the sake of brevity, but citations of sources have been retained and introductory material has been supplied to place the essays in a larger context.

We hope that these readings will aid students of American history in discovering the richness and diversity of the peoples of the United States and in understanding the origins of the racial problems which still plague the nation.

We wish to thank three people for their help in developing this volume: Richard J. Orsi for his suggestion of potential selections, Ann S. Jablin, our editor at Rand McNally, for her careful reading of the manuscript, and Pearlene V. Glasrud for her incisive and instructive comments as the work progressed.

Bruce A. Glasrud

Hayward, California   Alan M. Smith

Table of Contents

Table of Contents

Selected Bibliography

Index

Part I
Introduction

Introduction

Nonwhites in the United States comprise a substantial minority whose experience and life style differ significantly from that of the white majority. White Americans developed a social system in which race, color, and culture were important distinguishing criteria. With these factors as broad indicators of status in society, red, yellow, brown, or black skin marked a man as inferior in the eyes of the white majority and set limits on the extent to which he could share in the benefits of an expanding and upwardly mobile society.

As did the various white ethnic groups, nonwhites arrived in substantial blocs at specific junctures in the national development. There has been an increase in the population of nonwhites, although until recently Native Americans, called Indians because of a well-known mistake, were an exception. The population of Native Americans had declined as a result of incessant warfare, and in the process they lost much of their land, heritage, and livelihood. The first nonwhites to immigrate to North America were blacks from Africa who began to populate the continent at the same time as the Europeans since they were imported as slaves for profit-seeking whites. Even after the abolition of slavery, blacks faced a harsh caste system which severely regulated their lives.

The incorporation of other nonwhite groups awaited the mid-nineteenth century when the United States waged war against Mexico, conquered vast stretches of territory, and added to its population former citizens of her southern neighbor. Other Mexicans entered the United States as impoverished agricultural and industrial workers in the twentieth century, and, because of barriers created by language, culture, religion, and alien status, they were easily exploited.

Beginning in 1848, Chinese also entered the United States. They sought gold to take back to China; but racial and cultural differences again precluded equitable treatment, and they became poorly paid laborers. When some were able to achieve success despite the obstacles, alarmed whites brought about the enactment of the Chinese Exclusion Act. Other Orientals, Japanese, Filipinos, and Koreans, trailed the Chinese to the United States. Recently, additional minorities including Hawaiians, Eskimos, Puerto Ricans, and lesser numbers from Southeast Asia, India, and the Middle East have migrated to the United States.

Relations among the nonwhites varied with the predicament of each group. Often they competed with one another for the few menial positions or favors offered to minorities. At other times they joined forces against the white majority in a bid for privileges that were denied them. Some nonwhites strove for acceptance by the majority, which meant adopting white values, but usually they were restricted to separate and unequal areas where they developed their own cultures and societies apart from those of the whites.

Three themes stand out in the history of nonwhites in the United States. First, nonwhites confronted total domination by the white majority. Their subjugation took the forms of slavery, war, annihilation, physical torture, cultural deprivation, economic restriction, political exclusion, geographical removal, and social ostracism. Second, segregation became a way of life as the paramount white society forced physical separation upon them. Whenever the nonwhites sought apartheid, the whites, fearful of collective action directed against them, took reluctant steps to modify legal segregation. But there have been few meaningful steps toward integration, and the result remains in the confinement of blacks in ghettos, Chinese in Chinatowns, Chicanos in barrios, and Indians on reservations. Third, nonwhites resisted white encroachments. Their defiance assumed overt and covert forms, often at the same time. Overt resistance included riots, revolts, warfare, and murder; covert resistance often hid behind smiles, good behavior, and the signing of treaties. But dislike of whites and the white dominated society was obvious, even to those whites who insisted that nonwhites were happy with their second-class status.

The United States, a nation which has prided itself on its equalitarian nature, is, in actuality, a heterogeneous society that exhibits major schisms between the groups which comprise it. The tensions of American society are particularly apparent between the dominant white majority and the various nonwhite minorities. The nonwhites, subjugated, segregated, and defiant, remain a challenge to the nation's capacities for providing the promise of equality to all its citizens.

Accounts of the manner in which immigrants or minority groups
become, or fail to become, "Americanized" too often portray
the myths, rather than the realities, of that process. Milton M.
Gordon, in "Assimilation in America," asserts that Americans have
used three concepts to explain both what has happened and
what should happen to immigrants and the manner in which
newcomers have interacted with the dominant society: (1) Anglo-
conformity, (2) the melting pot, and (3) cultural pluralism.
Although cultural pluralism is the most accurate of the three, none
are apt descriptions of assimilation; rather, Gordon concludes,
the phrase "structural pluralism" better interprets the American
experience. In the United States acculturation which stresses
secondary and impersonal relationships takes place, but structural
assimilation which emphasizes primary and personal relationships is
often lacking. For racial minorities, however, even acculturation
has been limited. Instead, nonwhites have established separate
communities within the prevailing white society.

Assimilation in America: Theory and Reality

Milton M. Gordon

Three ideologies or conceptual models have competed for attention on the American scene as explanations of the way in which a nation, in the beginning largely white, Anglo-Saxon, and Protestant, has absorbed over 41 million immigrants and their descendants from variegated sources and welded them into the contemporary American people. These ideologies are Anglo-conformity, the melting pot, and cultural pluralism. They have served at various times, and often simultaneously, as explanations of what has happened—descriptive models—and of what should happen—goal models. Not infrequently they have been used in such a fashion that it is difficult to tell which of these two usages the writer has had in mind. In fact, one of the more remarkable omissions in the history of American intellectual thought is the relative lack of close analytical attention given to the theory of immigrant adjustment in the United States by its social scientists.

The result has been that this field of discussion—an overridingly

Abridged from Milton M. Gordon, "Assimilation in America: Theory and Reality," *Daedalus*, XC (1961), pp. 163–185. Reprinted by permission of *Daedalus*, Journal of the American Academy of Arts and Sciences, Boston, Mass., Spring 1961, *Ethnic Groups in American Life*. Some footnotes have been re-numbered.

important one since it has significant implications for the more familiar problems of prejudice, discrimination, and majority-minority group relations generally—has been largely preempted by laymen, representatives of belles lettres, philosophers, and apologists of various persuasions. Even from these sources the amount of attention devoted to ideologies of assimilation is hardly extensive. Consequently, the work of improving intergroup relations in America is carried out by dedicated professional agencies and individuals who deal as best they can with day-to-day problems of discriminatory behavior, but who for the most part are unable to relate their efforts to an adequate conceptual apparatus. Such an apparatus would, at one and the same time, accurately describe the present structure of American society with respect to its ethnic groups (I shall use the term "ethnic group" to refer to any racial, religious, or national origins collectively), and allow for a considered formulation of its assimilation or integration goals for the foreseeable future. One is reminded of Alice's distraught question in her travels in Wonderland: "Would you tell me, please, which way I ought to go from here?" "That depends a good deal," replied the Cat with irrefutable logic, "on where you want to get to."

The story of America's immigration can be quickly told for our present purposes. The white American population at the time of the Revolution was largely English and Protestant in origin, but had already absorbed substantial groups of Germans and Scotch-Irish and smaller contingents of Frenchmen, Dutchmen, Swedes, Swiss, South Irish, Poles, and a handful of migrants from other European nations. Catholics were represented in modest numbers, particularly in the middle colonies, and a small number of Jews were residents of the incipient nation. With the exception of the Quakers and a few missionaries, the colonists had generally treated the Indians and their cultures with contempt and hostility, driving them from the coastal plains and making the western frontier a bloody battleground where eternal vigilance was the price of survival.

Although the Negro at that time made up nearly one-fifth of the total population, his predominantly slave status, together with racial and cultural prejudice, barred him from serious consideration as an assimilable element of the society. And while many groups of European origin started out as determined ethnic enclaves, eventually, most historians believe, considerable ethnic intermixture within the white population took place. "People of different blood" [sic]—write two American historians about the colonial period, "English, Irish, German, Huguenot, Dutch, Swedish—mingled and intermarried with little thought of any difference."[1] In such a society, its people predominantly English, its white immigrants of other ethnic origins either English-speaking or derived largely from countries of northern and western Europe whose cultural divergences from the English were not great, and its dominant white population excluding by fiat the claims and considerations of welfare of the non-Caucasian minorities, the problem of assimilation understandably did not loom unduly large or complex.

The unfolding events of the next century and a half with increasing momentum dispelled the complacency which rested upon the relative simplicity of colonial and immediate post-Revolutionary conditions. The large-scale immigration to America of the famine-fleeing Irish, the Germans, and later the Scandinavians (along with additional Englishmen and other peoples of northern and western Europe) in the middle of the nineteenth century (the so-called "old immigration"), the emancipation of the Negro slaves and the problems created by post-Civil War reconstruction, the placing of the conquered Indian with his broken culture on government reservations, the arrival of the Oriental, first attracted by the discovery of gold and other opportunities in the West, and finally, beginning in the last quarter of the nineteenth century and continuing to the early 1920's, the swelling to proportions hitherto unimagined of the tide of immigration from the peasantries and "pales" of southern and eastern Europe—the Italians, Jews, and Slavs of the so-called "new immigration," fleeing the persecutions and industrial dislocations of the day—all these events constitute the background against which we may consider the rise of the theories of assimilation mentioned above. After a necessarily foreshortened description of each of these theories and their historical emergence, we shall suggest analytical distinctions designed to aid in clarifying the nature of the assimilation process, and then conclude by focusing on the American scene.

1. Allan Nevins and Henry Steele Commager, America: The Story of a Free People (Boston, Little, Brown, 1942), p. 58.

Anglo-Conformity

"Anglo-conformity"[2] is a broad term used to cover a variety of viewpoints about assimilation and immigration; they all assume the desirability of maintaining English institutions (as modified by the American Revolution), the English language, and English-oriented cultural patterns as dominant and standard in American life. However, bound up with this assumption are related attitudes. These may range from discredited notions about race and "Nordic" and "Aryan" racial superiority, together with the nativist political programs and exclusionist immigration policies which such notions entail, through an intermediate position of favoring immigration from northern and western Europe on amorphous, unreflective grounds ("They are more like us"), to a lack of opposition to any source of immigration, as long as these immigrants and their descendants duly adopt the standard Anglo-Saxon cultural patterns. There is by no means any necessary equation between Anglo-conformity and racist attitudes.

It is quite likely that "Anglo-conformity" in its more moderate aspects, however explicit its formulation, has been the most prevalent ideology of assimilation goals in America throughout the nation's history. . . .

Anglo-conformity received its fullest expression in the so-called Americanization movement which gripped the nation during World War I. While "Americanization" in its various stages had more than one emphasis, it was essentially a consciously articulated movement to strip the immigrant of his native culture and attachments and make him over into an American along Anglo-Saxon lines—all this to be accomplished with great rapidity. To use an image of a later day, it was an attempt at "pressure-cooking assimilation." It had prewar antecedents, but it was during the height of the world conflict that federal agencies, state governments, municipalities, and a host of private organizations joined in the effort to persuade the immigrant to learn English, take out naturalization papers, buy war bonds, forget his former origins and culture, and give himself over to patriotic hysteria.

2. The phrase is the Coles's. See Stewart G. Cole and Mildred Wiese Cole, *Minorities and the American Promise* (New York, Harper & Brothers, 1954), ch. 6.

After the war and the "Red scare" which followed, the excesses of the Americanization movement subsided. In its place, however, came the restriction of immigration through federal law. Foiled at first by presidential vetoes, and later by the failure of the 1917 literacy test to halt the immigrant tide, the proponents of restriction finally put through in the early 1920's a series of acts culminating in the well-known national-origins formula for immigrant quotas which went into effect in 1929. Whatever the merits of a quantitative limit on the number of immigrants to be admitted to the United States, the provisions of the formula, which discriminated sharply against the countries of southern and eastern Europe, in effect institutionalized the assumptions of the rightful dominance of Anglo-Saxon patterns in the land. Reaffirmed with only slight modifications in the Mc-Carran-Walter Act of 1952, these laws, then, stand as a legal monument to the creed of Anglo-conformity and a telling reminder that this ideological system still has numerous and powerful adherents on the American scene.

The Melting Pot

While Anglo-conformity in various guises has probably been the most prevalent ideology of assimilation in the American historical experience, a competing viewpoint with more generous and idealistic overtones has had its adherents and exponents from the eighteenth century onward. Conditions in the virgin continent, it was clear, were modifying the institutions which the English colonists brought with them from the mother country. Arrivals from non-English homelands such as Germany, Sweden, and France were similarly exposed to this fresh environment. Was it not possible, then, to think of the evolving American society not as a slightly modified England but rather as a totally new blend, culturally and biologically, in which the stocks and folkways of Europe, figuratively speaking, were indiscriminately mixed in the political pot of the emerging nation and fused by the fires of American influence and interaction into a distinctly new type?

Such, at any rate, was the conception of the new society which motivated that eighteenth-century French-born writer and agriculturalist, J. Hector St. John Crèvecoeur, who, after many years of

American residence, published his reflections and observations in *Letters from an American Farmer*.[3] Who, he asks, is the American?

> He is either an European, or the descendant of an European, hence that strange mixture of blood, which you find in no other country. I could point out to you a family whose grandfather was an Englishman, whose wife was Dutch, whose son married a French woman, and whose present four sons have now four wives of different nations. He is an American, who leaving behind him all his ancient prejudices and manners, receives new ones from the new mode of life he has embraced, the new government he obeys, and the new rank he holds. He becomes an American by being received in the broad lap of our great *Alma Mater*. Here individuals of all nations are melted into a new race of men, whose labours and posterity will one day cause great changes in the world.

Some observers have interpreted the open-door policy on immigration of the first three-quarters of the nineteenth century as reflecting an underlying faith in the effectiveness of the American melting pot, in the belief "that all could be absorbed and that all could contribute to an emerging national character."[4] ...

... Around the turn of the [twentieth] century the melting-pot idea became embedded in the ideals of the age as one response to the immigrant receiving experience of the nation. Soon to be challenged by a new philosophy of group adjustment ... and always competing with the more pervasive adherence to Anglo-conformity, the melting-pot image, however, continued to draw a portion of the attention consciously directed toward this aspect of the American scene in the first half of the twentieth century. In the mid-1940's a sociologist who had carried out an investigation of intermarriage trends in New Haven, Connecticut, described a revised conception of the melting process in that city and suggested a basic modification of the theory

---

3. J. Hector St. John Crèvecoeur, *Letters from an American Farmer* (New York, Albert and Charles Boni, 1925; reprinted from the 1st edn., London, 1782), pp. 54–55.

4. Oscar Handlin, ed., *Immigration as a Factor in American History* (Englewood, Prentice-Hall, 1959), p. 146.

of that process. In New Haven, Ruby Jo Reeves Kennedy[5] reported from a study of intermarriages from 1870 to 1940 that there was a distinct tendency for the British-Americans, Germans, and Scandinavians to marry among themselves—that is, within a Protestant "pool"; for the Irish, Italians, and Poles to marry among themselves— a Catholic "pool"; and for the Jews to marry other Jews. In other words, intermarriage was taking place across lines of nationality background, but there was a strong tendency for it to stay confined within one or the other of the three major religious groups, Protestants, Catholics, and Jews. Thus, declared Mrs. Kennedy, the picture in New Haven resembled a "triple melting pot" based on religious divisions, rather than a "single melting pot." Her study indicated, she stated, that "while strict endogamy is loosening, religious endogamy is persisting and the future cleavages will be along religious lines rather than along nationality lines as in the past. If this is the case, then the traditional 'single-melting-pot' idea must be abandoned, and a new conception, which we term the 'triple-melting-pot' theory of American assimilation, will take its place as the true expression of what is happening to the various nationality groups in the United States."[6] The triple-melting-pot thesis was later taken up by the theologian Will Herberg and formed an important sociological frame of reference for his analysis of religious trends in American society, *Protestant-Catholic-Jew.*[7] But the triple-melting-pot hypothesis patently takes us into the realm of a society pluralistically conceived. We turn now to the rise of an ideology which attempts to justify such a conception.

Cultural Pluralism

Probably all the non-English immigrants who came to American shores in any significant numbers from colonial times onward— settling either in the forbidding wilderness, the lonely prairie, or in

5. Ruby J. Reeves Kennedy, "Single or Triple Melting-Pot? Intermarriage Trends in New Haven, 1870–1940," *American Journal of Sociology*, 1944, 49:331–339. See also her "Single or Triple Melting-Pot? Intermarriage in New Haven, 1870–1950," *ibid.*, 1952, 58:56–59.

6. *Ibid.*, "Single or Triple Melting-Pot? . . . 1870–1940," p. 332 (author's italics omitted).

7. Will Herberg, *Protestant-Catholic-Jew* (Garden City, Doubleday, 1955).

some accessible urban slum—created ethnic enclaves and looked forward to the preservation of at least some of their native cultural patterns. Such a development, natural as breathing, was supported by the later accretion of friends, relatives, and countrymen seeking out oases of familiarity in a strange land, by the desire of the settlers to rebuild (necessarily in miniature) a society in which they could communicate in the familiar tongue and maintain familiar institutions, and, finally, by the necessity to band together for mutual aid and mutual protection against the uncertainties of a strange and frequently hostile environment. This was as true of the "old" immigrants as of the "new." In fact, some of the liberal intellectuals who fled to America from an inhospitable political climate in Germany in the 1830's, 1840's, and 1850's looked forward to the creation of an all-German state within the union, or, even more hopefully, to the eventual formation of a separate German nation, as soon as the expected dissolution of the union under the impact of the slavery controversy should have taken place.[8] Oscar Handlin, writing of the sons of Erin in mid-nineteenth-century Boston, recent refugees from famine and economic degradation in their homeland, points out: "Unable to participate in the normal associational affairs of the community, the Irish felt obliged to erect a society within a society, to act together in their own way. In every contact therefore the group, acting apart from other sections of the community, became intensely aware of its peculiar and exclusive identity."[9] Thus cultural pluralism was a fact in American society before it became a theory—a theory with explicit relevance for the nation as a whole, and articulated and discussed in the English-speaking circles of American intellectual life. . . .

The classic statement of the cultural pluralist position [appeared early in 1915 in two articles entitled] "Democracy versus the Melting-Pot." Their author was Horace Kallen, a Harvard-educated philos-

---

8. Nathan Glazer, "Ethnic Groups in America: From National Culture to Ideology," in Morroe Berger, Theodore Abel, and Charles H. Page, eds., *Freedom and Control in Modern Society* (New York, D. Van Nostrand, 1954), p. 161; Marcus Lee Hansen, *The Immigrant in American History* (Cambridge, Harvard University Press, 1940), pp. 129–140; John A. Hawgood, *The Tragedy of German-America* (New York, Putnam's, 1940), *passim*.

9. Oscar Handlin, *Boston's Immigrants* (Cambridge, Harvard University Press, 1959, rev. edn.), p. 176.

opher with a concern for the application of philosophy to societal affairs, and, as an American Jew, himself derivative of an ethnic background which was subject to the contemporary pressures for dissolution implicit in the "Americanization," or Anglo-conformity, and the melting-pot theories. In these articles Kallen vigorously rejected the usefulness of these theories as models of what was actually transpiring in American life or as ideals for the future. Rather he was impressed by the way in which the various ethnic groups in America were coincident with particular areas and regions, and with the tendency for each group to preserve its own language, religion, communal institutions, and ancestral culture. All the while, he pointed out, the immigrant has been learning to speak English as the language of general communication, and has participated in the overall economic and political life of the nation. These developments in which "the United States are in the process of becoming a federal state not merely as a union of geographical and administrative unities, but also as a cooperation of cultural diversities, as a federation or commonwealth of national cultures,"[10] the author argued, far from constituting a violation of historic American political principles, as the "Americanizers" claimed, actually represented the inevitable consequences of democratic ideals, since individuals are implicated in groups, and since democracy for the individual must by extension also mean democracy for his group.

The processes just described, however, as Kallen develops his argument, are far from having been thoroughly realized. They are menaced by "Americanization" programs, assumptions of Anglo-Saxon superiority, and misguided attempts to promote "racial" amalgamation. Thus America stands at a kind of cultural crossroads. It can attempt to impose by force an artificial, Anglo-Saxon oriented uniformity on its peoples, or it can consciously allow and encourage its ethnic groups to develop democratically, each emphasizing its particular cultural heritage. If the latter course is followed, as Kallen puts it at the close of his essay, then,[11]

10. Horace M. Kallen, "Democracy versus the Melting-Pot," *The Nation,* 18 and 25 February 1915; reprinted in his *Culture and Democracy in the United States,* Boni and Liveright, 1924; the quotation is on p. 116.
11. Kallen, *Culture and Democracy . . . ,* p. 124.

The outlines of a possible great and truly democratic commonwealth become discernible. Its form would be that of the federal republic; its substance a democracy of nationalities, cooperating voluntarily and autonomously through common institutions in the enterprise of self-realization through the perfection of men according to their kind. The common language of the commonwealth, the language of its great tradition, would be English, but each nationality would have for its emotional and involuntary life its own peculiar dialect or speech, its own individual and inevitable esthetic and intellectual forms. The political and economic life of the commonwealth is a single unit and serves as the foundation and background for the realization of the distinctive individuality of each *nation* that composes it and of the pooling of these in a harmony above them all. Thus "American civilization" may come to mean the perfection of the cooperative harmonies of "European civilization"—the waste, the squalor and the distress of Europe being eliminated—a multiplicity in a unity, an orchestration of mankind.

. . . In the twentieth century, particularly since World War II, "cultural pluralism" has become a concept which has worked its way into the vocabulary and imagery of specialists in intergroup relations and leaders of ethnic communal groups. In view of this new pluralistic emphasis, some writers now prefer to speak of the "integration" of immigrants rather than of their "assimilation."[12] However, with a few exceptions,[13] no close analytical attention has been given either by social scientists or practitioners of intergroup relations to the meaning of cultural pluralism, its nature and relevance for a modern industrialized society, and its implications for problems of prejudice

12. See W. D. Borrie et al., *The Cultural Integration of Immigrants* (a survey based on the papers and proceedings of the UNESCO Conference in Havana, April 1956), Paris, UNESCO, 1959; and William S. Bernard. "The Integration of Immigrants in the United States" (mimeographed), one of the papers for this conference.

13. See particularly Milton M. Gordon, "Social Structure and Goals in Group Relations"; and Nathan Glazer, "Ethnic Groups in America; From National Culture to Ideology," both articles in Berger, Abel, and Page, *op. cit.*; S. N. Eisenstadt, *The Absorption of Immigrants* (London, Routledge and Kegan Paul, 1954); and W. D. Borrie et al., *ibid.*

and discrimination—a point to which we referred at the outset of this discussion.

Conclusions

In the remaining pages I can make only a few analytical comments which I shall apply in context to the American scene, historical and current. My view of the American situation will not be documented here, but may be considered as a series of hypotheses in which I shall attempt to outline the American assimilation process.

First of all, it must be realized that "assimilation" is a blanket term which in reality covers a multitude of subprocesses. The most crucial distinction is one often ignored—the distinction between what I have elsewhere called "behavioral assimilation" and "structural assimilation."[14] The first refers to the absorption of the cultural behavior patterns of the "host" society. (At the same time, there is frequently some modification of the cultural patterns of the immigrant-receiving country, as well.) There is a special term for this process of cultural modification or "behavioral assimilation"—namely, "acculturation." "Structural assimilation," on the other hand, refers to the entrance of the immigrants and their descendants into the social cliques, organizations, institutional activities, and general civic life of the receiving society. If this process takes place on a large enough scale, then a high frequency of intermarriage must result. A further distinction must be made between, on the one hand, those activities of the general civic life which involve earning a living, carrying out political responsibilities, and engaging in the instrumental affairs of the larger community, and, on the other hand, activities which create personal friendship patterns, frequent home intervisiting, communal worship, and communal recreation. The first type usually develops so-called "secondary relationships," which tend to be relatively impersonal and segmental; the latter type leads to "primary relationships," which are warm, intimate, and personal.

With these various distinctions in mind, we may then proceed.

Built on the base of the original immigrant "colony" but frequently extending into the life of successive generations, the characteristic ethnic group experience is this: within the ethnic group there devel-

14. Milton M. Gordon, "Social Structure and Goals in Group Relations," p. 151.

ops a network of organizations and informal social relationships which permits and encourages the members of the ethnic group to remain within the confines of the group for all of their primary relationships and some of their secondary relationships throughout all the stages of the life cycle. From the cradle in the sectarian hospital to the child's play group, the social clique in high school, the fraternity and religious center in college, the dating group within which he searches for a spouse, the marriage partner, the neighborhood of his residence, the church affiliation and the church clubs, the men's and the women's social and service organizations, the adult clique of "marrieds," the vacation resort, and then, as the age cycle nears completion, the rest home for the elderly and, finally, the sectarian cemetery—in all these activities and relationships which are close to the core of personality and selfhood—the member of the ethnic group may if he wishes follow a path which never takes him across the boundaries of his ethnic structural network.

The picture is made more complex by the existence of social class divisions which cut across ethnic group lines just as they do those of the white Protestant population in America. As each ethnic group which has been here for the requisite time has developed second, third, or in some cases, succeeding generations, it has produced a college-educated group which composes an upper middle class (and sometimes upper class, as well) segment of the larger groups. Such class divisions tend to restrict primary group relations even further, for although the ethnic-group member feels a general sense of identification with all the bearers of his ethnic heritage, he feels comfortable in intimate social relations only with those who also share his own class background or attainment.

In short, my point is that, while *behavioral assimilation* or acculturation has taken place in America to a considerable degree, *structural assimilation*, with some important exceptions, has not been extensive.[15] The exceptions are of two types. The first brings us back to the "triple-melting-pot" thesis of Ruby Jo Reeves Kennedy and Will Herberg. The "nationality" ethnic groups have tended to merge within each of the three major religious groups. This has been particularly true of the Protestant and Jewish communities. Those

---

15. See Erich Rosenthal, "Acculturation without Assimilation?" *American Journal of Sociology*, 1960, 66:275–288.

descendants of the "old" immigration of the nineteenth century, who were Protestant (many of the Germans and all the Scandinavians), have in considerable part gradually merged into the white Protestant "subsociety." Jews of Sephardic, German, and Eastern-European origins have similarly tended to come together in their communal life. The process of absorbing the various Catholic nationalities, such as the Italians, Poles, and French Canadians, into an American Catholic community hitherto dominated by the Irish has begun, although I do not believe that it is by any means close to completion. Racial and quasi-racial groups such as the Negroes, Indians, Mexican-Americans, and Puerto Ricans still retain their separate sociological structures. The outcome of all this in contemporary American life is thus pluralism—but it is more than "triple" and it is more accurately described as *structural pluralism* than as cultural pluralism, although some of the latter also remains.

My second exception refers to the social structures which implicate intellectuals. There is no space to develop the issue here, but I would argue that there is a social world or subsociety of the intellectuals in America in which true structural intermixture among persons of various ethnic backgrounds, including the religious, has markedly taken place.

My final point deals with the reasons for these developments. If structural assimilation has been retarded in America by religious and racial lines, we must ask why. The answer lies in the attitudes of both the majority and the minority groups and in the way these attitudes have interacted. A saying of the current day is, "It takes two to tango." To apply the analogy, there is no good reason to believe that white Protestant America has ever extended a firm and cordial invitation to its minorities to dance. Furthermore, the attitudes of the minority-group members themselves on the matter have been divided and ambiguous. Particularly for the minority religious groups, there is a certain logic in ethnic communality, since there is a commitment to the perpetuation of the religious ideology and since structural intermixture leads to intermarriage and the possible loss to the group of the intermarried family. Let us, then, examine the situation serially for various types of minorities.

With regard to the immigrant, in his characteristic numbers and socioeconomic background, structural assimilation was out of the question. He did not want it, and he had a positive need for the comfort of his own communal institutions. The native American, moreover, whatever the implications of his public pronouncements, had no intention of opening up his primary group life to entrance by these hordes of alien newcomers. The situation was a functionally complementary standoff.

The second generation found a much more complex situation. Many believed they heard the siren call of welcome to the social cliques, clubs, and institutions of white Protestant America. After all, it was simply a matter of learning American ways, was it not? Had they not grown up as Americans, and were they not culturally different from their parents, the "greenhorns"? Or perhaps an especially eager one reasoned (like the Jewish protagonist of Myron Kaufmann's novel, *Remember Me To God*, aspiring to membership in the prestigious club system of Harvard undergraduate social life) "If only I can go the last few steps in Ivy League manners and behavior, they will surely recognize that I am one of them and take me in." But, alas, Brooks Brothers suit notwithstanding, the doors of the fraternity house, the city men's club, and the country club were slammed in the face of the immigrant's offspring. That invitation was not really there in the first place; or, to the extent it was, in Joshua Fishman's phrase, it was a " 'look me over but don't touch me' invitation to the American minority group child."[16] And so the rebuffed one returned to the homelier but dependable comfort of the communal institutions of his ancestral group. There he found his fellows of the same generation who had never stirred from the home fires. Some of these had been too timid to stray; others were ethnic ideologists committed to the group's survival; still others had never really believed in the authenticity of the siren call or were simply too passive to do more than go along the familiar way. All could now join in the task that was well within the realm of the sociologically possible—the build-up of social institutions and organizations within the ethnic enclave, manned increasingly by members of the second generation and suitably separated by social class.

Those who had for a time ventured out gingerly or confidently, as the case might be, had been lured by the vision of an "American"

16. Joshua A. Fishman, "Childhood Indoctrination for Minority-Group Membership and the Quest for Minority-Group Biculturism in America," in Oscar Handlin, ed., *Group Life in America* (Cambridge, Harvard University Press, forthcoming).

social structure that was somehow larger than all subgroups and was ethnically neutral. Were they, too, not Americans? But they found to their dismay that at the primary group level a neutral American social structure was a mirage. What at a distance seemed to be a quasi-public edifice flying only the all-inclusive flag of American nationality turned out on closer inspection to be the clubhouse of a particular ethnic group—the white Anglo-Saxon Protestants, its operation shot through with the premises and expectations of its parental ethnicity. In these terms, the desirability of whatever invitation was grudgingly extended to those of other ethnic backgrounds could only become a considerably attenuated one.

With the racial minorities, there was not even the pretense of an invitation. Negroes, to take the most salient example, have for the most part been determinedly barred from the cliques, social clubs, and churches of white America. Consequently, with due allowance for internal class differences, they have constructed their own network of organizations and institutions, their own "social world." There are now many vested interests served by the preservation of this separate communal life, and doubtless many Negroes are psychologically comfortable in it, even though at the same time they keenly desire that discrimination in such areas as employment, education, housing, and public accommodations be eliminated. However, the ideological attachment of Negroes to their communal separation is not conspicuous. Their sense of identification with ancestral African national cultures is virtually nonexistent, although Pan-Africanism engages the interest of some intellectuals and although "black nationalist" and "black racist" fringe groups have recently made an appearance at the other end of the communal spectrum. As for their religion, they are either Protestant or Catholic (overwhelmingly the former). Thus, there are no "logical" ideological reasons for their separate communality; dual social structures are created solely by the dynamics of prejudice and discrimination, rather than being reinforced by the ideological commitments of the minority itself.

Structural assimilation, then, has turned out to be the rock on which the ships of Anglo-conformity and the melting pot have foundered. To understand that behavioral assimilation (or acculturation) without massive structural intermingling in primary relationships has been the dominant motif in the American experience of creating and developing a nation out of diverse peoples is to comprehend the most essential sociological fact of that experience. It is against the background of "structural pluralism" that strategies of strengthening intergroup harmony, reducing ethnic discrimination and prejudice, and maintaining the rights of both those who stay within and those who venture beyond their ethnic boundaries must be thoughtfully devised.

Part II
Clash of Cultures,
1607-1763

Clash of Cultures, 1607–1763

On the eve of the American Revolution the thirteen British North American colonies contained approximately two-and-a-half-million people, the majority of whom were whites of European origin. Over 60 percent of the white inhabitants were of English stock, and English institutions and culture dominated the society of the colonies. There were also two sizeable nonwhite minorities, red and black, which lived within the colonies but outside the framework of the dominant European culture.

Indians were a majority when the English first established permanent North American settlements. In the early seventeenth century nearly one million Indians inhabited the area which became the United States. The English, deriving their first ideas about American colonization from reports of the Spanish experience, expected to encounter tractable Indians who could easily be subdued and relegated to the status of servants and slaves. Initial contacts with Indians quickly dashed such expectations. The Indians tolerated the white intruders as a harmless and unimpressive minority. Later they resisted the increasing number of Europeans as a threat to Indian land and culture. The English, on the other hand, refused to acknowledge Indian culture and engaged in weak and sporadic efforts to incorporate the red men into their civilization, mainly through religious proselytization. The Indians generally spurned such advances.

The steady growth of English population and a pattern of settlement which relied heavily on agriculture to provide an economic raison d'être for the colonies created continual clashes between whites and Indians over the use and possession of land. On some occasions the whites secured land by sale and treaty. When Indians were unwilling to relinquish the land, warfare often followed. The results of persistent white aggression were disastrous for the Indians. Some nations were driven west beyond the frontier of white settlement, often into the territory of hostile Indian rivals. Other tribes, such as the Pequots of Connecticut, were annihilated by the whites. Still others made their peace with the whites; they were frequently absorbed by the English society in a subservient and segregated position. This latter result led to the rapid modification of Indian culture. Despite some concerted efforts to retake the land, such as King Philip's War in Massachusetts (1675–76), the Indians were unable to stem the white tide. Technological superiority, increasing numbers, and a more acquisitive attitude toward land insured white domination.

The other nonwhite minority in British North America, the blacks, began to arrive a decade after the founding of Virginia when twenty Africans were brought to Jamestown in 1619 by a Dutch slave trader and sold to white settlers as bound servants. The forced immigration of Africans to the colonies continued on a very limited scale throughout the seventeenth century, but accelerated with the development of commercial agriculture in the southern colonies as white planters sought new sources of labor. White indentured servants proved to be an expensive, unruly, and often inefficient labor force, and the relationship which developed between the English and the Indians prevented, in most cases, the development of red slavery. By the midseventeenth century white masters in Virginia and Maryland began to experiment with black labor, and the laws of these colonies reflected the concurrent development of a slave system. Toward the end of the century the expansion of the African slave trade, the rapid growth of American plantation agriculture, and the decline of competing slave markets in the West Indies combined to assure the large scale importation and enslavement of Africans in the southern colonies. Blacks constituted a large portion of the population in every colony from Maryland south by mid-eighteenth century, and almost all were enslaved by a system of perpetual servitude which gave masters virtually unlimited authority over their lives and labor.

While both minorities, red and black, lived within the American colonies, they were not in any real sense a part of the white culture or society. Socially, legally, and physically, they existed apart from and subservient to the white majority.

Nancy Oestreich Lurie,
*"Indian Cultural Adjustment
to European Civilization"*

Conflict between Indians and whites has been a persistent theme
in American history. Although this racial antagonism is often
presented as a simple economic struggle over occupation of the land,
Nancy Lurie, in "Indian Cultural Adjustment to European
Civilization," demonstrates that much more was involved. The
sections of Professor Lurie's article, which appear here, cover the
early years of Indian-white relationships in the first permanent
English colony in North America and reveal a clash of cultures
which led to the supremacy of one at the expense of the other.
Particularly significant is the author's observation that upon initial
contact the two cultures were different but not unequal. Yet,
initiating a pattern which would appear many times in American
history, white Virginians succeeded in destroying the Powhatan
Confederacy in less than four decades.

Indian Cultural Adjustment to European Civilization

Nancy Oestreich Lurie

...During much of the sixteenth century Europeans were active in regions immediately adjacent to Virginia and possibly in Virginia itself. Their activity was often associated with violence, and there was sufficient time for rumors concerning them to have reached the Virginia natives before any direct contacts were made. By the time the English attempted to found colonies on the east coast toward the close of the sixteenth century, they encountered difficulties which may have been more than the simple result of European inexperience in developing techniques for survival in the New World. Raleigh's enterprise, for example, may have been singulary ill-timed. A general unrest in Indian-white relationships marked the period from 1577 to 1597 in the Carolina region where Raleigh's followers chose to remain. Pemisipan, a Secotan chief who attempted to organize opposition to the British in 1585, could hardly have been blamed if he saw a curious similarity to accounts he may have heard concerning the Spanish when, for the trifling matter of the theft

Abridged from Nancy Oestreich Lurie, "Indian Cultural Adjustment to European Civilization," *Seventeenth-Century America: Essays in Colonial History,* edited by James Morton Smith (Chapel Hill: University of North Carolina Press, 1959), pp. 33–60. Reprinted by permission of the publisher and the Institute of Early American History and Culture. Footnotes have been renumbered.

of a silver cup, the English burned the corn and destroyed the buildings at his village of Aquascogoc.[1]

The later events at Cape Henry, the first landfall of the Jamestown colonists, suggest that the immediate hostility expressed by the Indians was inspired by fear of reprisals for the fate of Raleigh's colony. The Indians who attacked the English belonged to the Chesapeake tribe, immediately adjacent to the tribes with whom Pemisipan conspired.[2] It is also possible, as James Mooney implies, that by 1607 the Virginia Indians evaluated any sudden appearance of Europeans as evil and took immediate measures to repel them. However, this view oversimplifies several important factors. Long before any Europeans arrived at Jamestown, the Indians had been fighting over matters of principle important to them, such as possession of land and tribal leadership. If they were aware of the fate of other Indians at the hands of Europeans, there was no reason for them to assume that their fate would be similar; they were not necessarily allied with the beleaguered tribes, nor did they share a sense of racial kinship. Sharp cultural differences and even sharper linguistic differences separated the various Indian societies. While there was reason to fear and hate the Europeans as invaders who made indiscriminate war on all Indians, the fear was only that of being taken unawares and the hate could be modified if the tribes which had fallen victim thus far were strangers or even enemies. If the Indians of Virginia had any knowledge of Europeans, they must have been aware that the white men were fundamentally outnumbered, frequently unable to support themselves in an environment which the Indians found eminently satisfactory, and that European settlements were usually short lived. The appearance of the English was probably far less alarming than 350 years of hindsight indicate ought to have been the case.

This is demonstrated by the fact that the Virginia Indians under

1. Maurice A. Mook, "Algonkian Ethnohistory of the Carolina Sound," *Jour. of The Washington Academy of Sciences*, 34 (1944), 185–86, quotes and discusses the journal of 1585, usually attributed to Sir Richard Grenville, regarding this incident and also establishes the location of Aquascogoc in North Carolina.

2. [George Percy], "Observations gathered out of *A Discourse of the Plantation of the Southerne Colonie in Virginia by the English, 1606*; written by that Honorable Gentleman, Master George Percy," in Edward Arber, ed., *Captain John Smith . . . Works, 1608–1631* (Birmingham, Eng., 1884), xl–li.

the leadership of Powhatan seem to have made their first adjustments to Europeans in terms of existing native conditions.[3] Primary among these conditions were Powhatan's efforts to gain firmer control over his subject tribes and to fight tribes traditionally at enmity with his followers. It was expedient to help the settlers stay alive, for they could be useful allies in his established plans; but at the same time he could not allow them to gain ascendancy. The situation was complicated by factionalism in Powhatan's ranks and lack of accord among the settlers. However, recognition of the fundamental aboriginal situation makes the early events at Jamestown understandable on a rational basis. It offers a logical foundation for subsequent developments in Indian-white relationships and Indian adjustments to European civilization as the result of something more than barbaric cupidity and a thirst for the white man's blood.

Certainly a wary sensitivity to any sign of hostility or treachery characterized the behavior of both whites and Indians at the outset of settlement at Jamestown. The Europeans were still seriously concerned about the probable fate of Raleigh's colony and they had already been attacked by the Indians at Cape Henry. The Indians, in turn, may well have possessed information concerning the alarmingly retributive temperament of Europeans, at least in terms of the incident at nearby Aquascogoc, if not through generalized opinions derived from the long history of intermittent European contact along the east coast.

Nevertheless, the party of Europeans that set out on exploration of the country about Jamestown encountered a welcome at the various Indian villages different from the greetings offered at Cape Henry. Except for one cold but not overtly hostile reception in the Weanoc country, the white men were feted, fed, and flattered. At the same time a suggestion of the uncertainty of the next years occurred before the exploring party had even returned to their head-

---

3. There are many data to indicate that in culture contact situations, generally regular processes of cultural acceptance and rejection can be traced to the formulation of analogies between innovations and existing phenomena on the part of the recipient culture. See Melville J. Herskovits, Man and His Works (New York, 1950), 553–58, for a discussion of the processes of reinterpretation and syncretism; Ralph Linton, The Study of Man (New York, 1936), 317–18, and Homer G. Barnett, "Cultural Processes," Amer. Anthropologist, 42 (1940), 21–48, give similar but independent analyses of analogy formulation on the basis of form, function, meaning, and use or principle of given traits.

quarters—at Jamestown the remaining colonists were attacked by a party of local Indians.[4] Events of this nature as well as the general observations recorded during the first two years at Jamestown are particularly instructive in any attempt to understand Indian motivations and policy regarding the British.

The narratives are difficult to follow because of the variety of orthographies employed for Indian words. Certain features remain speculative because initial communication between whites and Indians was limited to the use of signs and the few native words that could be learned readily.[5] However, it is possible to see native culture in terms of regularities and consistencies which were not obvious to the colonists. Likewise, the apparent inconsistencies on the part of the natives, recounted by the settlers as innate savage treachery, indicate that the aboriginal culture was in a process of growth, elaboration, and internal change. These phases of culture, which included both extensive tendencies of intertribal confederation and divisive reactions expressed by individual tribes, were interrupted and redirected but not initiated by the arrival of Europeans in 1607.

From the viewpoint of the twentieth century, it is difficult to realize that the material differences between the Indians and the European colonists, who lived before the full development of the industrial revolution, were equalled if not outweighed by the similarities of culture. This was especially true in Virginia, where a local florescence of culture and a demonstrated ability to prevail over other tribes gave the Indians a sense of strength which blinded them to the enormity of the threat posed by the presence of Europeans. There was actually little in the Europeans' imported bag of tricks which the Indians could not syncretize with their own experience. Metal was not unknown to them: they used native copper, brought in from the West, for decorative purposes. Metal weapons and domestic utensils were simply new and effective forms of familiar objects to accomplish familiar tasks. Even guns were readily mas-

---

4. [Captain Gabriel Archer], "A Relayton of the Discovery &c. 21 May–22 June, 1607," in Arber, ed., Works of John Smith, li–lii. It is worth noting that news of the attack was apparently communicated to the Indians who were entertaining the exploring party, but that Powhatan had either been unable to prevent the attack or had not known of the plan until it was accomplished.

5. Throughout the present study, spelling of Indian words, apart from direct quotations, has been regularized according to the pattern of Mook's publications.

tered after the noise, which evoked astonishment at first, was understood as necessary to their operation. Likewise, fabrics and articles of personal adornment were part of Indian technology. Many utilitarian objects such as nets, weirs, and gardening implements were very similar in both Indian and European culture. European ships were simply larger and different, as was fitting for a people interested in traveling greater distances by open water than the Indians had ever cared to do.

Expansive accounts of the size and permanence of the great European cities could easily have been likened by the natives to the impressive aboriginal developments in the lower Mississippi Valley; archeological evidence suggests that knowledge of this cultural complex was widespread.[6] Even if these Indian models of nascent urbanization are discounted, the statements made by Europeans about their country and king may well have sounded like the exaggerations of outnumbered strangers endeavoring to buttress their weaknesses with talk of powerful but distant brothers. This explanation is admittedly conjectural, although we find ample documentation of the Indians' disinclination to admit any significant superiority in white culture at a somewhat later period. During the early nineteenth century, when the industrial revolution was underway and the eastern United States was heavily populated by whites, Indian visitors were brought from the West in the hope that they would be cowed by the white man's power and cease resistance to the forces of civilization. The Indians remained singularly unimpressed.[7] Furthermore, at the time Jamestown was founded in the seventeenth century, the only knowledge Indians possessed concerning Europeans indicated that Indians were well able to oppose white settlement. Raleigh's ill-fated colony was a clear reminder of the European's mortality.

6. Paul Martin, George Quimby, and Donald Collier, *Indians Before Columbus* (Chicago, 1947), offer useful illustrations of the far-flung continental diffusion of cultural traits in prehistoric times, although dates assigned have been reassessed during the last ten years.

7. See Katherine C. Turner, *Red Men Calling on the Great White Father* (Norman, Okla., 1951), which presents a series of essays on such visits. Although the Indians considered their trips as entertaining educational experiences, their quoted remarks in the main reveal opinions that the white man had an unnecessarily complex and burdensome way of life at the expense of the finer one enjoyed by the Indians.

Although the early accounts tend to take a patronizing view of the Indians, the points on which the Europeans felt superior had little meaning for the aborigines: literacy, different sexual mores, ideas of modesty, good taste in dress and personal adornment, and Christian religious beliefs. The argument of technological superiority at that time was a weak one; despite guns and large ships the Europeans could not wrest a living from a terrain which, by Indian standards, supported an exceptionally large population. Scientific knowledge of generally predictable group reactions thus suggests that the degree of ethnocentrism was probably equal on both sides of the contact between Indians and Europeans in Virginia. Recognition of the Indians' self-appraisal is necessary for a clear understanding of their basis of motivation and consequent behavior in relation to Europeans.

Moreover, it was evident to the colonists that they were dealing with a fairly complex society, exhibiting many characteristics of leadership, social classes, occupational specialization, social control, and economic concepts that were eminently comprehensible in European terms. If the exploring parties overstated the case when they translated *weroance* as "king" and likened tribal territories to European kingdoms, they at least had a truer understanding of the nature of things than did the democratic Jefferson, who first designated the Virginia tribes as the "Powhatan Confederacy."[8] Since the term "Confederacy" is so firmly entrenched in the literature, it will be retained here as a matter of convenience; but, in reality, Powhatan was in the process of building something that approximated an empire. By 1607 it was not an accomplished fact, but the outlines were apparent....

...The Chesapeake Indians are included in the Confederacy, but this southernmost group was not fully under Powhatan's control at the time the settlers arrived. Their attack on the colonists at Cape Henry gave Powhatan the opportunity to gain favor with the English by swiftly avenging the hostile action. Although some historians have implied that Powhatan destroyed the entire tribe, it is far more

8. John Smith observed that "one as Emperour ruleth over many kings or governours." *A Map of Virginia with a Description of the Countrey* ... and *The General Historie of Virginia* ..., in Arber, ed., *Works of John Smith*, 79, 375. Mook, "Aboriginal Population of Tidewater Virginia," *Amer. Anthropologist*, 44 (1944), 197, attributes the first use of the term "Powhatan Confederacy" to Jefferson.

likely that he simply killed the leaders and placed trusted kinsmen in these positions.[9]

Powhatan's method of fighting and his policy of expanding political control combined a reasoned plan of action with quick ferocity and a minimum of bloodshed. Indian warfare was generally limited to surprise attacks and sniping from cover. Constant replacements of fighting men kept the enemy occupied and wore down their resistance, while actual casualties were relatively limited in number. Accounts of Powhatan's conquests and the occurrences observed after 1607 point to a carefully devised method of establishing his control over a wide territory. Entire communities might be killed if they proved exceptionally obstinate in rendering homage and paying tribute, but in most cases Powhatan simply defeated groups of questionable loyalty and upon their surrender moved them to areas where he could keep better watch over them. Trusted members of the Confederacy were then sent to occupy the vacated regions, while Powhatan's relatives were distributed throughout the tribes in positions of leadership.[10] Mook's studies indicate that the degree of Powhatan's leadership decreased in almost direct proportion to the increase in geographical distance between the Pamunkey and the location of a given tribe.[11] Throughout the entire region, however, the combination of ample sustenance, effective techniques of production, provident habits of food storage, and distribution of supplies through exchange offset shortcomings in the political framework connecting the tribes and helped to cement social ties and produce a commonality of culture. . . .

. . . At the outset of colonization in 1607 Powhatan's policies can best be understood in relation to circumstances antedating the arrival of the Jamestown settlers. Powhatan saw the whites in his territory as potential allies and as a source of new and deadly weapons to be used in furthering his own plans for maintaining control over his Confederacy and protecting the Confederacy as a whole against the

9. [Archer], "Relayton," Arber, ed., *Works of John Smith*, xliv; William Strachey, *The Historie of Travaile into Virginia Britannia*, Hakluyt Society edn. (London, 1849), 101, 105; James Mooney, "Powhatan Confederacy," *Amer. Anthropologist*, 9 (1907), 130.

10. Mooney, "Powhatan Confederacy," *Amer. Anthropologist*, 9 (1907), 136.

11. Mook, "Virginia Ethnology from an Early Relation," *Wm. and Mary College Qtly.*, 2nd ser., 23 (1943), 115.

threat posed by the alien tribes of the piedmont region. Likewise, existing concepts of intertribal trade in foodstuffs and other commodities were extended to include trade with the newly arrived whites. It is worth noting that European novelties, apart from weapons, were of far less interest to Powhatan than the fact that the British possessed copper, an object vested with traditional native values and heretofore obtained with great difficulty.[12]

In the initial stages of contact between the Indians and the whites, therefore, it is hardly surprising that Powhatan and his people felt at least equal to the English. The chieftain could appreciate the foreigners as allies in the familiar business of warfare and trade, but in general there seemed little to emulate in European culture and much to dislike about the white men. However, even in the most difficult phases of their early relationship, Powhatan did not indulge in a full-scale attack against the settlers. At that time he was still engaged in strengthening his Confederacy and perhaps he could not risk extensive Indian defection to the side of the whites. But there is an equal likelihood that Powhatan's primary motivation was the desire to control and use the whites for his own purposes rather than to annihilate them.

At the time Jamestown was founded, native civilization was enjoying a period of expansion, and Powhatan had ample reason for sometimes considering the English as more an annoyance than a serious danger. The unusually rich natural environment and the security offered by the Confederacy stimulated the growth of social institutions and cultural refinements. In addition, the Virginia Indians were exceptionally powerful and, by aboriginal standards, their population was large: the entire Confederacy numbered some 8,500 to 9,000 people, or a density of approximately one person to every square mile.[13] The Indians lived according to a well-ordered and impressively complex system of government. They dwelled in secure

---

12. "Their manner of trading is for copper, beads, and such like; for which they giue such commodities as they haue, as skins, fowle, fish, flesh, and their country corne." Arber, ed., *Works of John Smith. Ibid.*, 74, 369. Smith reported that Powhatan requested him to abandon the settlement among the Paspehegh and move to his own country: "Hee promised to giue me Corne, Venison, or what I wanted to feede vs: Hatchets and Copper wee should make him, and none should disturb vs." *Ibid.*, 20.

13. Mook, "Aboriginal Population," *Amer. Anthropologist*, 44 (1944), 201, 208.

villages, had substantial houses and extensive gardens, and had a notable assemblage of artifacts for utilitarian, religious, and decorative purposes.

The Indians won the grudging respect of the colonists for their advanced technology, but the Europeans were contemptuous of their seemingly hopeless commitment to superstition, while their ceremonialism appeared to the whites a ridiculous presumption of dignity.[14] A typical bias of communication between Europeans and Indians is seen in Smith's account of the Quiyoughcohannock chief who begged the settlers to pray to the Christian God for rain because their own deities had not fulfilled the Indians' requests. Smith asserted that the Indians appealed to the whites because they believed the Europeans' God superior to their own, just as the Europeans' guns were superior to bows and arrows. Yet Smith notes with some wonder that the Quiyoughcohannock chief, despite his cordiality and interest in the Christian deity, could not be prevailed upon to "forsake his false Gods."[15] Actually this chief of one of the lesser tribes of the Confederacy illustrated the common logic of polytheistic people who often have no objection to adding foreign deities to their pantheon if it seems to assure more efficient control of the natural universe. The chief was not interested in changing his religious customs in emulation of the Europeans; he merely wished to improve his own culture by judicious borrowing—a gun at one time, a supernatural being at another.

Nor would the chief have dared respond to a new religion in its entirety, even if such an unlikely idea had occurred to him. The whole structure of tribal life relied upon controlling the mysterious aspects of the world by a traditional body of beliefs which required the use of religious functionaries, temples, idols, and rituals. These were awesome arrangements and not to be treated lightly, although improvement by minor innovations might be permitted.[16]

14. [Archer], "Relayton," Arber, ed., *Works of John Smith*, 1, provides a characteristic response of the colonists in his description of Opechancanough, who "so set his Countenance stryving to be stately, as to our seeming he became a fool."

15. Arber, ed., *Works of John Smith*, 79, 374.

16. For a general account of religion derived from the basic sources, see Charles C. Willoughby, "The Virginia Indians of the Seventeenth Century," *Amer. Anthropologist*, 9 (1907), 61–63. The most complete single account in the early narratives based on firsthand observation is included in Henry Spelman, "Relation of Virginea," 1613, in Arber, ed., *Works of John Smith*, cv–cvi.

The geopolitical sophistication of the Virginia tribes is reflected in the secular hierarchy of leadership which extended in orderly and expanding fashion from the villages, through the separate tribes, up to Powhatan as head of the entire Confederacy. A gauge of the complexity of government is the fact that the Confederacy shared with the Europeans such niceties of civilization as capital punishment.[17] In small societies having a precarious economy, indemnities in goods or services are usually preferred to taking the life of a culprit even in crimes as serious as murder. However, where the life of the offender or one of his kinsmen is exacted for the life of the victim, punishment is the concern of the particular families involved; the rest of the group merely signifies approval of the process as a means of restoring social equilibrium after an offense is committed. Powhatan's government, however, was much closer to that of the English than it was to many of the tribes of North America. Punishment was meted out by a designated executioner for an offense against the society as the society was symbolized in the person of the leader.

Nevertheless, despite its elaborate civil structure, the Confederacy exhibited a universal rule of any society: a complex theory of government does not necessarily assure complete success in application. Powhatan not only had unruly subjects to deal with, but entire tribes in his domain could not be trusted. Relations between whites and Indians therefore were always uncertain, largely because of political developments within the Confederacy. When the colonists were supported by Powhatan, they were in mortal danger from those dissatisfied tribes of the Confederacy which had the foresight to realize that the English might one day assist Powhatan to enforce his authority. When Powhatan and his closest associates turned upon the settlers, the less dependable tribes became friendly to the whites.

In view of this morass of political allegiances, it is little wonder that early accounts of the settlers are replete with material which seems to prove the innate treachery of the Indians. Yet the militant phases of Indian activity, as illustrated by the initial attack on Jamestown and Powhatan's vengeance on the offending Chesapeake tribe, must be seen as part of a larger policy involving alternative methods of settling inter-group differences. Although the settlers knew that

17. Arber, ed., *Works of John Smith*, 81–82, 377–78; Spelman, "Relation," *ibid.*, cxi.

dissatisfaction among Powhatan's followers offered a means of preventing a coordinated Indian attack, they also discovered that established mechanisms of diplomacy existed among the Indians that could be employed for their benefit. For example, the Jamestown settlement was located in the territory of the Paspahegh tribe, and relations with this tribe frequently became strained. The Powhatan forces represented by the leaders of the Pamunkey, Arrohattoc, Youghtanund, and Mattaponi offered to act as intermediaries in negotiating peace with the Paspehegh and other hostile tribes or, if necessary, to join forces with the settlers in an armed assault on mutual enemies.[18]

If the Europeans found it difficult to live among the Indians, the Europeans seemed equally unpredictable to the Indians. Early in his relationship with the English, Powhatan was promised five hundred men and supplies for a march on the Monacan and Manahoac; but instead of finding wholehearted support among his allies for this campaign, Powhatan discovered that the whites were helpless to support themselves in the New World. As time wore on and they became increasingly desperate for food, the Europeans were less careful in the difficult business of trying to distinguish friends from enemies. They extorted supplies promiscuously, driving hard bargains by the expedient of burning villages and canoes.[19]

It is problematical whether, as Smith implies, Powhatan was actually unable to destroy the handful of English because he could not organize his tribes for a full-scale offensive or whether he was biding his time in the hope of eventually establishing a clear-cut power structure in which the colonists would be allowed to survive but remain subservient to his designs in native warfare. At any rate, after two years of English occupation at Jamestown, Powhatan moved from his traditional home on the Pamunkey River some fifteen miles from the Europeans and settled in a more remote village upstream on the Chickahominy River. Violence flared periodically during

18. [Archer], "Relayton," *ibid.*, lv.
19. See Mooney, "Powhatan Confederacy," *Amer. Anthropologist,* 9 (1907), 136–39, for an exhaustive review of instances illustrating the ever harsher measures taken by the colonists in coercing the Indians. In his indignation, Mooney scarcely notes that the Indians took measures of revenge by killing whites so that the process of hostilities increased over a period of time, with each side intent on settling some score with the other side.

these early years: colonists were frequently killed and often captured. Sometimes, being far from united in their allegiance, they fled to the Indian villages, where they were usually well treated. Captives and runaways were exchanged as hostages when one side or the other found it convenient. However, if Powhatan was willing to take advantage of dissident feeling among the whites, he was no fool and he finally put to death two colonists who seemed to be traitors to both sides at the same time. The execution was much to Smith's satisfaction, for it saved him from performing the task and assured a far more brutal punishment than he would have been able to inflict upon the renegades.[20]

Throughout the period from 1607 to 1609, the chronicles include a complexity of half-told tales involving alliances and enmities and mutual suspicions, of Indians living among settlers and settlers living among Indians. Although this interaction was of an individual nature, the two groups learned something of each other; yet each side maintained its own values and traditions as a social entity. The Indians were primarily concerned with obtaining new material goods. By theft, trade, and the occupation of European artisans in their villages, they increased their supply of armaments and metal work. With the use of Indian guides and informants, the settlers became familiar with the geography of the region, and they also learned the secrets of exploiting their new environment through techniques of native gardening. For the most part, however, conscious efforts to bridge the cultural gap were unavailing. There was one amusing attempt to syncretize concepts of Indian and European monarchy and thereby bring about closer communication, when Powhatan was treated to an elaborate "coronation." The chief weroance was only made more vain by the ceremonies; he was by no means transformed into a loyal subject of the English sovereign, as the white settlers had intended.[21]

An increasing number of settlers arrived in Virginia and, with the

20. Smith admitted that Powhatan's move to the village of Orapaks was simply to get away from the settlers. Arber, ed., Works of John Smith, 20, 70–71, 366–67; for the execution, see ibid., 487.

21. Ibid., 124–25, 434–35. Smith's disgust was aroused by the coronation because it not only made Powhatan conceited, but it threatened to disrupt the trade in copper. Powhatan had been willing to exchange huge amounts of corn for a pittance, and Smith feared he would be spoiled by the rich coronation gifts.

help of Indians who by this time had ample reason to let the whites perish, managed to weather the hazards of the "starving time." As the whites became more firmly established, competition between Europeans and Indians took on the familiar form of a struggle for land. Armed clashes occurred frequently, but there were no organized hostilities, and the Indians continued to trade with the English. A peace which was formally established in 1614 and lasted until 1622 is often attributed to a refinement of Powhatan's sensibilities because of the marriage of Pocahontas and John Rolfe. Although Pocahontas was indeed the favorite child of Powhatan, it is likely that the chieftain's interest in her marriage was not entirely paternal. This strengthening of the social bond between Indians and Europeans helped solidify Powhatan's power and prestige among the confederated tribes, as he was thus enduringly allied with the whites.

Continuation of harmony between Indians and whites for a period of eight years was doubtless rendered possible because enough land still remained in Virginia for both settlers and Indians to live according to their accustomed habits. The seriousness of the loss of Indian land along the James River was lessened by the existence of a strip of virtually unoccupied territory just east of the fall line which ran the length of the Confederacy's holdings. If properly armed and not disturbed by internal dissensions and skirmishes with the English, the Powhatan tribes could afford to settle at the doorstep of their piedmont neighbors and even hope to expand into enemy territory. Hostilities require weapons, and peaceful trade with the English meant easier access to arms which the Confederacy could turn against the Monacan and Manahoac. It is also possible that by this time Powhatan realized the vast strength of the English across the sea and was persuaded to keep the settlers as friends. Knowledge of Europe would have been available to the chieftain through such Indians as Machumps, described by William Strachey as having spent "somtym in England" as well as moving "to and fro amongst us as he dares and as Powhatan gives him leave."[22]

Whatever were Powhatan's reasons for accepting the peace, it appears that he utilized the lull in hostilities to unify the Confederacy and deal with his traditional enemies. We have no direct evidence of activities against the piedmont tribes, for there is little

22. Strachey, *Historie of Travaile into Virginia*, 54.

historical data regarding the western area at this time. However, by the time the fur trade became important in the West the Monacan and Manahoac had lost the power which had once inspired fear among the tribes of the Confederacy. In view of Powhatan's years of scheming and the probable closer proximity of the Confederacy to the piedmont region after 1614, it may be conjectured that the Virginia chieftain and his people took some part in the downfall of the Monacan and Manahoac.[23]

When Powhatan died in 1618, his brother Opechancanough succeeded him as leader of the Confederacy.[24] Opechancanough continued to observe Powhatan's policy of peace for four years, although relations between Indians and Europeans were again degenerating. The Indians' natural resources were threatened as the increasing tobacco crops encroached on land where berries had grown in abundance and game had once been hunted. In the face of European advance, the Indians became restive and complained of the settlers' activities; but these signs went unnoticed by the colonists.[25] Opechancanough was aware that the real danger to the Confederacy arose from neither internal dissensions nor traditional Indian enemies but from the inexorable growth of European society in Virginia. He was apparently able to convince all the member tribes of this fact, if they had not already drawn their own conclusions. The subsequent uprising of 1622 was a well-planned shock to the English; it was

23. Throughout the accounts of 1607–8 there are references to aiding Powhatan in dealing with the piedmont Siouans and Powhatan's satisfaction in the promises. Arber, ed., *Works of John Smith*, 20, 70–71, 366–67; [Archer], "Relayton," *ibid.*, xlvii. As relations between Powhatan and the settlers became strained, Powhatan discouraged the settlers from going to the Monacan, fearing that the whites might ally themselves with his enemies. Smith quotes Powhatan: "As for the Monacans, I can revenge my own iniuries." *Ibid.*, 124, and see 482–83. For the subsequent decline of the Monacan, see the journal of Batt's expedition reprinted from the British Museum manuscript in Bushnell, "Discoveries Beyond the Appalachian Mountains in September, 1671," *Amer. Anthropologist*, 9 (1907), 46–53.

24. Arber, ed., *Works of John Smith*, 451; Robert Beverley, *The History and Present State of Virginia*, ed. by Louis B. Wright (Chapel Hill, 1947), 61.

25. Edward D. Neill, *History of the Virginia Company of London* (Albany, N. Y., 1869), 317–19, cites references which suggest that the Indians expressed excessive protestations of kindness and friendship in order to lull the settlers' suspicions in 1622. Shortly after Powhatan's death, however, fear of the Indians was so intense that Captain Spelman was harshly dealt with on the belief that he was engaged in inciting the Indians to hostile acts.

alarming not so much for the destruction wrought, since by that time the Europeans could sustain the loss of several hundred people, but for the fact that the Confederacy could now operate as a unified fighting organization. This was a solidarity which Powhatan either had been unable or was disinclined to achieve.

Doubtless Opechancanough expected reprisals, but he was totally unprepared for the unprecedented and utter devastation of his lands and the wholesale slaughter of his people. The tribes were scattered, some far beyond the traditional boundaries of their lands, and several of the smaller groups simply ceased to exist as definable entities. Gradually as the fury of revenge died down, the remnants of the Confederacy regrouped and began to return to their homelands. However, the settlers were no longer complacent about their Indian neighbors. In addition to campaigning against the natives, they erected a string of fortifications between Chesiac and Jamestown, and they tended to settle Virginia in the south rather than toward the north and west.[26] In effect, therefore, Opechancanough accomplished a limited objective; a line was established between Indians and Europeans, but the line was only temporary and the Indians paid a terrible price.

Moreover, the cultural gap widened during the ensuing years. Following the period of reprisals the Indians were left to make a living and manage their affairs as best they could. Many old grievances seemed to be forgotten, and the natives gave the appearance of accepting their defeat for all time. Opechancanough, who had eluded capture immediately after the attack of 1622, remained at large, but the Europeans attempted to win tribes away from his influence rather than hunt him down at the risk of inflaming his followers. Finally, white settlement once more began to spread beyond the safety of concentrated colonial population. Tensions were re-created on the frontier, and there were minor skirmishes; the Indians complained to the English, but they also continued their trading activities. Thus matters continued for more than twenty years until large-scale hostilities again broke out.[27]

The uprising of 1644 was surprisingly effective. It is generally

26. Mook, "Aboriginal Population," *Amer. Anthropologist*, 44 (1944), 204–5, discusses shifts in Indian tribal populations as a response to European movements after 1622.

27. Edward D. Neill, *Virginia Calororum: The Colony under the Rule of Charles the First and Second, A.D. 1625–A.D. 1685* (Albany, N. Y., 1886), 60–61.

known that in both the 1622 and the 1644 uprisings the percentage of Indians killed in relation to the total Indian population was far greater than the percentage of settlers killed in relation to the total white population. Yet with far fewer Indians to do the fighting, Opechancanough managed to kill at least as many Europeans in the second attack as he had in the first.[28] The uprising is another proof that the Indians' method of adjusting to changes wrought by the Europeans continued to be an attempt to prevail over or remove the source of anxiety—the settlers—rather than to adapt themselves to the foreign culture. Certainly the Indians never felt that their difficulties would be resolved by assimilation among the whites, a solution which the colonists at times hoped to effect through the adoption of Indian children, intermarriage, and Indian servitude.[29]

Hopeless though the uprising appears in retrospect, it was entirely logical within Opechancanough's own cultural frame of reasoning. It is impossible to determine whether the Indians were aware of the futility of their action, nor do we know enough about the psychology of these people to ascribe to them such a grim fatalism that they would prefer a quick and honorable death to the indignities of living in subjection to the whites. But there is something impressive about Opechancanough, an old and enfeebled man, being carried on a litter to the scene of battle. Whatever the outcome his days were numbered. His young warriors, however, knew of the horrible reprisals of 1622 and they understood the cost of being defeated by the white man. Yet they too were willing to risk an all-out attack.

There is little doubt that Opechancanough realized the danger inherent in rebellion. He was a shrewd strategist and a respected leader. It is entirely possible that he hoped for assistance from forces outside the Confederacy. Tension had existed between the whites of Virginia and Maryland for a number of years, and in one instance the Virginians had hoped to incite the Confederacy against their neighbors. Maryland had been settled only ten years before the second uprising, and although hostile incidents between whites and Indians had occurred, her Indian policy had been more just and humane than Virginia's. If Opechancanough did expect military

28. Mooney, "Powhatan Confederacy," *Amer. Anthropologist*, 9 (1907), 138–39, discusses reductions in Indian population. Opechancanough's secrecy inspires wonder, but the success of the attack is indicative of the degree of separation that marked the lives of the colonists and the Indians by 1644.

29. Neill, *Virginia Calororum*, 74.

assistance from whites for his uprising against whites, he had historical precedent to inspire him. Powhatan had exploited factionalism among the Jamestown settlers, and it may be that the tension between Virginia and Maryland suggested an extension of his policy to Opechancanough. Whatever the motivations behind Opechancanough's design for rebellion, the second uprising attested to the strength of the old Confederacy and indicated clearly the stubborn resistance of the Indians to cultural annihilation.

Although the usual revenge followed the attack of 1644, Virginia's Indian policy was beginning to change. The Powhatan tribes were too seriously reduced in numbers to benefit greatly by the progress, but their treatment at the hands of the colonists following the uprising marked a new development in Indian-white relations, one which eventually culminated in the modern reservation system. In 1646 a formal treaty was signed with the Powhatan Confederacy establishing a line between Indian and white lands and promising the Indians certain rights and protection in their holdings. While their movements were to be strictly regulated, the natives were guaranteed recognition for redress of wrongs before the law. There were two particularly important features of the treaty. First, the Indians were to act as scouts and allies against the possibility of outside tribes' invading the colony; this policy was in contrast to the earlier device of attempting to win the friendship of peripheral tribes to enforce order among the local Indians.[30] Second, and consistent with the growing importance of the fur trade in colonial economics, the Indians were to pay a tribute each year in beaver skins. During the following years various legislative acts were adopted to protect the Indians in their rights and establish mutual responsibilities with the tribes.[31]

30. As early as 1609, the instructions given Thomas Gates as acting governor of the colony indicate the initial policy decided upon: "If you make friendship with any of thiese nations as you must doe, choose to do it with those that are farthest from you & enemies unto those amongst whom you dwell for you shall have least occasion to have differences with them, and by that means a surer league of amity." The entire text of Gates's instructions as they related to the Indians is quoted in Bushnell, "Virginia From Early Records," *Amer. Anthropologist*, 9 (1907), 35.

31. See Wesley Frank Craven, *The Southern Colonies in the Seventeenth Century, 1607–1689* (Baton Rouge, La., 1949), 361–66, for a discussion of changes in Virginia's Indian policy.

Winthrop D. Jordan,
*"Modern Tensions
and the Origins of American Slavery"*

The conflict between blacks and whites in the United States has caused many scholars to search American history for the origins of racial prejudice. In "Modern Tensions and the Origins of American Slavery," Winthrop Jordan reports on the arguments of earlier historians. Most scholars had followed one of two theses: that slavery was responsible for the growth of prejudice, or that prejudice led to the institution of slavery. Jordan emphasized that the history of white racism in America is inextricably bound to the development of slavery, but the causal relationship is less certain. He concludes that the institution of slavery and white prejudice toward blacks developed gradually and simultaneously, each factor reinforcing the other. In a subsequent work, White Over Black, Jordan found conclusive evidence to indicate a jaundiced English view of black Africans even before contact between them was established. The resulting entrenchment of both slavery and racism by the eighteenth century fixed the pattern of black subjugation which has been an enduring theme of American history.

Modern Tensions
and the Origins of American Slavery
Winthrop D. Jordan

Thanks to John Smith we know that Negroes first came to the
British continental colonies in 1619.[1] What we do not know is
exactly when Negroes were first enslaved there. This question has
been debated by historians for the past seventy years, the critical
point being whether Negroes were enslaved almost from their first
importation or whether they were at first simply servants and only
later reduced to the status of slaves. The long duration and vigor of
the controversy suggest that more than a simple question of dating
has been involved. In fact certain current tensions in American
society have complicated the historical problem and greatly heightened its significance. Dating the origins of slavery has taken on a
striking modern relevance.

Winthrop D. Jordan, "Modern Tensions and the Origins of American Slavery,"
Journal of Southern History, XXVIII (February, 1962), pp. 18–30. Copyright ©
1962 by the Southern Historical Association. Reprinted by permission of the
Managing Editor. A modified and much more complete description of the origin
of American slavery is in Winthrop D. Jordan, *White Over Black: American
Attitudes Toward the Negro, 1550–1812* (Chapel Hill, 1968).

1. "About the last of August came in a dutch man of warre that sold us twenty
Negars." Smith was quoting John Rolfe's account. Edward Arber and A. G.
Bradley (eds.), *Travels and Works of Captain John Smith* ... (2 vols., Edin-
burgh, 1910), II, 541.

During the nineteenth century historians assumed almost universally that the first Negroes came to Virginia as slaves. So close was their acquaintance with the problem of racial slavery that it did not occur to them that Negroes could ever have been anything but slaves. Philip A. Bruce, the first man to probe with some thoroughness into the early years of American slavery, adopted this view in 1896, although he emphasized that the original difference in treatment between white servants and Negroes was merely that Negroes served for life. Just six years later, however, came a challenge from a younger, professionally trained historian, James C. Ballagh. His *A History of Slavery in Virginia* appeared in the *Johns Hopkins University Studies in Historical and Political Science*, an aptly named series which was to usher in the new era of scholarly detachment in the writing of institutional history. Ballagh offered a new and different interpretation; he took the position that the first Negroes served merely as servants and that enslavement did not begin until around 1660, when statutes bearing on slavery were passed for the first time.[2]

There has since been agreement on dating the statutory establishment of slavery, and differences of opinion have centered on when enslavement began in actual practice. Fortunately there has also been general agreement on slavery's distinguishing characteristics: service for life and inheritance of like obligation by any offspring. Writing on the free Negro in Virginia for the Johns Hopkins series, John H. Russell in 1913 tackled the central question and showed that some Negroes were indeed servants but concluded that "between 1640 and 1660 slavery was fast becoming an established fact. In this twenty years the colored population was divided, part being servants and part being slaves, and some who were servants defended themselves with increasing difficulty from the encroachments of slavery."[3] Ulrich B. Phillips, though little interested in the matter, in 1918 accepted Russell's conclusion of early servitude and transition toward slavery after 1640. Helen T. Catterall took much the same position in 1926.

2. Philip A. Bruce, *Economic History of Virginia in the Seventeenth Century* (2 vols., New York, 1896), II, 57–130; James C. Ballagh, *A History of Slavery in Virginia* (Baltimore, 1902), 28–35.

3. John H. Russell, *The Free Negro in Virginia, 1619–1865* (Baltimore, 1913), 29.

On the other hand, in 1921 James M. Wright, discussing the free Negro in Maryland, implied that Negroes were slaves almost from the beginning, and in 1940 Susie M. Ames reviewed several cases in Virginia which seemed to indicate that genuine slavery had existed well before Ballagh's date of 1660.[4]

All this was a very small academic gale, well insulated from the outside world. Yet despite disagreement on dating enslavement, the earlier writers—Bruce, Ballagh, and Russell—shared a common assumption which, though at the time seemingly irrelevant to the main question, has since proved of considerable importance. They assumed that prejudice against the Negro was natural and almost innate in the white man. It would be surprising if they had felt otherwise in this period of segregation statutes, overseas imperialism, immigration restriction, and full-throated Anglo-Saxonism. By the 1920's, however, with the easing of these tensions, the assumption of natural prejudice was dropped unnoticed. Yet only one historian explicitly contradicted that assumption: Ulrich Phillips of Georgia, impressed with the geniality of both slavery and twentieth-century race relations, found no natural prejudice in the white man and expressed his "conviction that Southern racial asperities are mainly superficial, and that the two great elements are fundamentally in accord."[5]

Only when tensions over race relations intensified once more did the older assumption of natural prejudice crop up again. After World War II American Negroes found themselves beneficiaries of New Deal politics and reforms, wartime need for manpower, worldwide repulsion at racist excesses in Nazi Germany, and growingly successful colored anticolonialism. With new militancy Negroes

---

4. *Ibid.*, 23–39; Ulrich B. Phillips, *American Negro Slavery* (New York, 1918), 75–77, and *Life and Labor in the Old South* (Boston, 1929), 170; Helen T. Catterall (ed.), *Judicial Cases Concerning American Slavery and the Negro* (5 vols., Washington, 1926–1937), I, 54–55, 57–63; James M. Wright, *The Free Negro in Maryland, 1634–1860* (New York, 1921), 21–23; Susie M. Ames, *Studies of the Virginia Eastern Shore in the Seventeenth Century* (Richmond, 1940), 100–106. See also T. R. Davis, "Negro Servitude in the United States," *Journal of Negro History*, VIII (July 1923), 247–83, and Edgar T. Thompson, "The Natural History of Agricultural Labor in the South" in David K. Jackson (ed.), *American Studies in Honor of William Kenneth Boyd* (Durham, N. C., 1940), 127–46.

5. Phillips, *American Negro Slavery*, viii.

mounted an attack on the citadel of separate but equal, and soon it became clear that America was in for a period of self-conscious reappraisal of its racial arrangements. Writing in this period of heightened tension (1949) a practiced and careful scholar, Wesley F. Craven, raised the old question of the Negro's original status, suggesting that Negroes had been enslaved at an early date. Craven also cautiously resuscitated the idea that white men may have had natural distaste for the Negro, an idea which fitted neatly with the suggestion of early enslavement. Original antipathy would mean rapid debasement.[6]

In the next year (1950) came a sophisticated counterstatement, which contradicted both Craven's dating and implicitly any suggestion of early prejudice. Oscar and Mary F. Handlin in "Origins of the Southern Labor System" offered a case for late enslavement, with servitude as the status of Negroes before about 1660. Originally the status of both Negroes and white servants was far short of freedom, the Handlins maintained, but Negroes failed to benefit from increased freedom for servants in mid-century and became less free rather than more.[7] Embedded in this description of diverging status were broader implications: Late and gradual enslavement undercut the possibility of natural, deep-seated antipathy toward Negroes. On the contrary, if whites and Negroes could share the same status of half freedom for forty years in the seventeenth century, why could they not share full freedom in the twentieth?

The same implications were rendered more explicit by Kenneth M. Stampp in a major reassessment of Southern slavery published two years after the Supreme Court's 1954 school decision. Reading physiology with the eye of faith, Stampp frankly stated his assumption "that innately Negroes are, after all, only white men with black skins, nothing more, nothing less."[8] Closely following the Handlins' article on the origins of slavery itself, he almost directly denied any pattern of early and inherent racial antipathy: "... Negro and white

6. Wesley F. Craven, *The Southern Colonies in the Seventeenth Century, 1607–1689* (Baton Rouge, 1949), 217–19, 402–403.

7. *William and Mary Quarterly*, s. 3, VII (April 1950), 199–222.

8. Kenneth M. Stampp, *The Peculiar Institution: Slavery in the Ante-Bellum South* (New York, 1956), vii–viii, 3–33.

servants of the seventeenth century seemed to be remarkably uncon-
cerned about their visible physical differences." As for "the trend toward special treatment" of the Negro, "physical and cultural differences provided handy excuses to justify it."[9] Distaste for the Negro,
then, was in the beginning scarcely more than an appurtenance of
slavery.

These views squared nicely with the hopes of those even more
directly concerned with the problem of contemporary race relations,
sociologists and social psychologists. Liberal on the race question almost to a man, they tended to see slavery as the initial cause of the
Negro's current degradation. The modern Negro was the unhappy
victim of long association with base status. Sociologists, though unin-
terested in tired questions of historical evidence, could not easily
assume a natural prejudice in the white man as the cause of slavery.
Natural or innate prejudice would not only violate their basic assumptions concerning the dominance of culture but would under-
mine the power of their new Baconian science. For if prejudice was
natural there would be little one could do to wipe it out. Prejudice
must have followed enslavement, not vice versa, else any liberal program of action would be badly compromised. One prominent social
scientist suggested in a UNESCO pamphlet that racial prejudice in
the United States commenced with the cotton gin![10]

Just how closely the question of dating had become tied to the
practical matter of action against racial prejudice was made apparent
by the suggestions of still another historian. Carl N. Degler grappled
with the dating problem in an article frankly entitled "Slavery and
the Genesis of American Race Prejudice."[11] The article appeared in

9. *Ibid.*, 21–22.

10. Arnold Rose, "The Roots of Prejudice" in UNESCO, *The Race Question
in Modern Science* (New York, 1956), 224. For examples of the more general
view see Frederick G. Detweiler, "The Rise of Modern Race Antagonisms,"
American Journal of Sociology, XXXVII (March 1932), 743; M. F. Ashley
Montagu, *Man's Most Dangerous Myth: The Fallacy of Race* (New York, 1945),
10–11, 19–20; Gunnar Myrdal, *An American Dilemma: The Negro Problem and
Modern Democracy* (New York, 1944), 83–89, 97; Paul Kecskemeti, "The Psychological Theory of Prejudice: Does it Underrate the Role of Social History?"
Commentary, XVIII (October 1954), 364–66.

11. *Comparative Studies in Society and History*, II (October 1959), 49–68. See
also Degler, *Out of Our Past: The Forces that Shaped Modern America* (New
York, 1959), 26–39.

1959, a time when Southern resistance to school desegregation seemed more adamant than ever and the North's hands none too clean, a period of discouragement for those hoping to end racial discrimination. Prejudice against the Negro now appeared firm and deep-seated, less easily eradicated than had been supposed in, say, 1954. It was Degler's view that enslavement began early, as a result of white settlers' prejudice or antipathy toward the first Negroes. Thus not only were the sociologists contradicted but the dating problem was now overtly and consciously tied to the broader question of whether slavery caused prejudice or prejudice caused slavery. A new self-consciousness over the American racial dilemma had snatched an arid historical controversy from the hands of an unsuspecting earlier generation and had tossed it into the arena of current debate.

Ironically there might have been no historical controversy at all if every historian dealing with the subject had exercised greater care with facts and greater restraint in interpretation. Too often the debate entered the realm of inference and assumption. For the crucial early years after 1619 there is simply not enough evidence to indicate with any certainty whether Negroes were treated like white servants or not. No historian has found anything resembling proof one way or the other. The first Negroes were sold to the English settlers, yet so were other Englishmen. It can be said, however, that Negroes were set apart from white men by the word Negroes, and a distinct name is not attached to a group unless it is seen as different. The earliest Virginia census reports plainly distinguished Negroes from white men, sometimes giving Negroes no personal name; and in 1629 every commander of the several plantations was ordered to "take a generall muster of all the inhabitants men woemen and Children as well Englishe as Negroes."[12] Difference, however, might or might not involve inferiority.

The first evidence as to the actual status of Negroes does not appear until about 1640. Then it becomes clear that some Negroes were serving for life and some children inheriting the same obligation. Here it is necessary to suggest with some candor that the Handlins'

---

12. H. R. McIlwaine (ed.), *Minutes of the Council and General Court of Colonial Virginia, 1622–1632, 1670–1676* (Richmond, 1924), 196. See the lists and musters of 1624 and 1625 in John C. Hotten (ed.), *The Original Lists of Persons of Quality . . .* (New York, 1880), 169–265.

statement to the contrary rests on unsatisfactory documentation.[13] That some Negroes were held as slaves after about 1640 is no indication, however, that American slavery popped into the world fully developed at that time. Many historians, most cogently the Handlins, have shown slavery to have been a gradual development, a process not completed until the eighteenth century. The complete deprivation of civil and personal rights, the legal conversion of the Negro into a chattel, in short slavery as Americans came to know it, was not accomplished overnight. Yet these developments practically and logically depended on the practice of hereditary lifetime service, and it is certainly possible to find in the 1640's and 1650's traces of slavery's most essential feature.[14]

The first definite trace appears in 1640 when the Virginia General Court pronounced sentence on three servants who had been retaken after running away to Maryland. Two of them, a Dutchman and a Scot, were ordered to serve their masters for one additional year and then the colony for three more, but "the third being a negro named John Punch shall serve his said master or his assigns for the time of his natural life here or else where." No white servant in America, so

13. "The status of Negroes was that of servants; and so they were identified and treated down to the 1660's." ("Origins," 203.) The footnote to this statement reads, "For disciplinary and revenue laws in Virginia that did not discriminate Negroes from other servants, see Hening, *Statutes*, I, 174, 198, 200, 243, 306 (1631–1645)." But pp. 200 and 243 of William Waller Hening (ed.), *The Statutes at Large; Being a Collection of All the Laws of Virginia . . .* (2nd ed. of vols. 1–4, New York, 1823), I, in fact contain nothing about either servants or Negroes, while a tax provision on p. 242 specifically discriminates against Negro women. The revenue act on p. 306 lists the number of pounds of tobacco levied on land, cattle, sheep, horses, etc., and on tithable persons, and provides for collection of lists of the above so that the colony can compute its tax program; nothing else is said of servants and tithables. To say, as the Handlins did in the same note, that Negroes, English servants, and horses, etc., were listed all together in some early Virginia wills, with the implication that Negroes and English servants were regarded as alike in status, is hardly correct unless one is to assume that the horses were sharing this status as well. (For complete bibliographical information on Hening [ed.], *Statutes*, see E. G. Swem, *Virginia Historical Index* [2 vols., Roanoke, Va., 1934–1936], I, xv–xvi.)

14. Latin-American Negroes did not lose all civil and personal rights, did not become mere chattels, yet we speak of "slavery" in Latin America without hesitation. See Frank Tannenbaum, *Slave and Citizen: The Negro in the Americas* (New York, 1947), and Gilberto Freyre, *The Masters and the Slaves: A Study in the Development of Brazilian Civilization* (New York, 1946).

far as is known, ever received a like sentence.[15] Later the same month a Negro was again singled out from a group of recaptured runaways; six of the seven were assigned additional time while the Negro was given none, presumably because he was already serving for life.[16] After 1640, too, county court records began to mention Negroes, in part because there were more of them than previously—about two per cent of the Virginia population in 1649.[17] Sales for life, often including any future progeny, were recorded in unmistakable language. In 1646 Francis Pott sold a Negro woman and boy to Stephen Charlton "to the use of him ... forever." Similarly, six years later William Whittington sold to John Pott "one Negro girle named Jowan; aged about Ten yeares and with her Issue and produce duringe her (or either of them) for their Life tyme. And their Successors forever"; and a Maryland man in 1649 deeded two Negro men and a woman "and all their issue both male and Female." The executors of a York County estate in 1647 disposed of eight Negroes— four men, two women, and two children—to Captain John Chisman "to have hold occupy posesse and inioy and every one of the afforementioned Negroes forever[.]"[18] The will of Rowland Burnham of "Rapahanocke," made in 1657, dispensed his considerable number of Negroes and white servants in language which clearly differentiated between the two by specifying that the whites were to serve for their "full terme of tyme" and the Negroes "for ever."[19] Nor did anything

---

15. "Decisions of the General Court," *Virginia Magazine of History and Biography*, V (January 1898), 236. Abbot Emerson Smith in the standard work on servitude in America, *Colonists in Bondage: White Servitude and Convict Labor in America, 1607–1776* (Chapel Hill, 1947), 171, says that "there was never any such thing as perpetual slavery for any white man in any English colony." There were instances in the seventeenth century of white men sold into "slavery," but this was when the meaning of the term was still indefinite and often equated with servitude.

16. "Decisions of the General Court," 236–37.

17. *A Perfect Description of Virginia* ... (London, 1649), reprinted in Peter Force (ed.), *Tracts* ... (4 vols., Washington, 1836–1846), II.

18. These four cases may be found in Northampton County Deeds, Wills &c. (Virginia State Library, Richmond), No. 4 (1651–1654), 28 (misnumbered 29), 124; *Archives of Maryland* (69 vols., Baltimore, 1883–1961), XLI, 261–62; York County Records (Virginia State Library), No. 2 (transcribed Wills & Deeds, 1645–1649), 256–57.

19. Lancaster County Loose Papers (Virginia State Library), Box of Wills, 1650–1719, Folder 1656–1659.

in the will indicate that this distinction was exceptional or novel.

In addition to these clear indications that some Negroes were owned for life, there were cases of Negroes held for terms far longer than the normal five or seven years.[20] On the other hand, some Negroes served only the term usual for white servants, and others were completely free.[21] One Negro freeman, Anthony Johnson, himself owned a Negro.[22] Obviously the enslavement of some Negroes did not mean the immediate enslavement of all.

Further evidence of Negroes serving for life lies in the prices paid for them. In many instances the valuations placed on Negroes (in estate inventories and bills of sale) were far higher than for white servants, even those servants with full terms yet to serve. Since there was ordinarily no preference for Negroes as such, higher prices must have meant that Negroes were more highly valued because of their greater length of service. Negro women may have been especially prized, moreover, because their progeny could also be held perpetually. In 1645, for example, two Negro women and a boy were sold for 5,500 pounds of tobacco. Two years earlier William Burdett's inventory listed eight servants (with the time each had still to serve) at valuations ranging from 400 to 1,100 pounds, while a "very antient" Negro was valued at 3,000 and an eight-year-old Negro girl at 2,000 pounds, with no time-remaining indicated for either. In the late 1650's an inventory of Thomas Ludlow's large estate evaluated a white servant with six years to serve at less than an elderly Negro man and only one half of a Negro woman.[23] The labor owned by James Stone in 1648 was evaluated as follows:

20. For examples running for as long as thirty-five years, see *William and Mary Quarterly*, s. 1, XX (October 1911), 148; Russell, *Free Negro in Virginia*, 26–27; Ames, *Eastern Shore*, 105. Compare the cases of a Negro and an Irish servant in *Calendar of Virginia State Papers* ... (11 vols., Richmond, 1875–1892), I, 9–10, and *Maryland Archives*, XLI, 476–78; XLIX, 123–24.

21. Russell, *Free Negro in Virginia*, 24–41. See especially the cases in *Virginia Magazine of History and Biography*, V (July 1897), 40; York County Deeds, Wills, Orders, etc. (Virginia State Library), No. 1 (1633–1657, 1691–1694), 338–39.

22. John H. Russell, "Colored Freemen As Slave Owners in Virginia," *Journal of Negro History*, I (July 1916), 234–37.

23. York County Records, No. 2, 63; Northampton County Orders, Deeds, Wills, &c., No. 2 (1640–1645), 224; York County Deeds, Orders, Wills, &c. (1657–1662), 108–109.

	lb tobo
Thomas Groves, 4 yeares to serve	1300
Francis Bomley for 6 yeares	1500
John Thackstone for 3 yeares	1300
Susan Davis for 3 yeares	1000
Emaniell a Negro man	2000
Roger Stone 3 yeares	1300
Mingo a Negro man	2000[24]

Besides setting a higher value on the two Negroes, Stone's inventory, like Burdett's, failed to indicate the number of years they had still to serve. It would seem safe to assume that the time remaining was omitted in this and similar documents simply because the Negroes were regarded as serving for an unlimited time.

The situation in Maryland was apparently the same. In 1643 Governor Leonard Calvert agreed with John Skinner, "mariner," to exchange certain estates for seventeen sound Negro "slaves," fourteen men and three women between sixteen and twenty-six years old. The total value of these was placed at 24,000 pounds of tobacco, which would work out to 1,000 pounds for the women and 1,500 for the men, prices considerably higher than those paid for white servants at the time.[25]

Wherever Negro women were involved, however, higher valuations may have reflected the fact that they could be used for field work while white women generally were not. This discrimination between Negro and white women, of course, fell short of actual enslavement. It meant merely that Negroes were set apart in a way clearly not to their advantage. Yet this is not the only evidence that Negroes were subjected to degrading distinctions not directly related to slavery. In several ways Negroes were singled out for special treatment which suggested a generalized debasing of Negroes as a group. Significantly, the first indications of debasement appeared at about the same time as the first indications of actual enslavement.

The distinction concerning field work is a case in point. It first

24. York County Records, No. 2, 390.

25. Apparently Calvert's deal with Skinner was never consummated. *Maryland Archives*, IV, vii, 189, 320–21. For prices of white servants see *ibid.*, IV, 31, 47–48, 74, 78–79, 81, 83, 92, 98, 108–109, 184, 200, 319.

appeared on the written record in 1643, when Virginia pointedly recognized it in her taxation policy. Previously tithable persons had been defined (1629) as "all those that worke in the ground of what qualitie or condition soever." Now the law stated that all adult men and Negro women were to be tithable, and this distinction was made twice again before 1660. Maryland followed a similar course, beginning in 1654.[26] John Hammond, in a 1656 tract defending the tobacco colonies, wrote that servant women were not put to work in the fields but in domestic employments, "yet som wenches that are nasty, and beastly and not fit to be so imployed are put into the ground."[27] Since all Negro women were taxed as working in the fields, it would seem logical to conclude that Virginians found them "nasty" and "beastly." The essentially racial nature of this discrimination was bared by a 1668 law at the time slavery was crystallizing on the statute books:

> Whereas some doubts have arisen whether negro women set free were still to be accompted tithable according to a former act, *It is declared by this grand assembly* that negro women, though permitted to enjoy their ffreedome yet ought not in all respects to be admitted to a full fruition of the exemptions and impunities of the English, and are still lyable to payment of taxes.[28]

Virginia law set Negroes apart in a second way by denying them the important right and obligation to bear arms. Few restraints could indicate more clearly the denial to Negroes of membership in the white community. This action, in a sense the first foreshadowing of the slave codes, came in 1640, at just the time when other indications first appear that Negroes were subject to special treatment.[29]

26. Hening (ed.), *Statutes*, I, 144, 242, 292, 454. The Handlins erroneously placed the "first sign of discrimination" in this matter at 1668 ("Origins," 217n). For Maryland, see *Maryland Archives*, I, 342; II, 136, 399, 538–39; XIII, 538–39.
27. John Hammond, *Leah and Rachel, or, the Two Fruitful Sisters Virginia, and Mary-land: Their Present Condition, Impartially Stated and Related . . .* (London, 1656), reprinted in Force (ed.), *Tracts*, II.
28. Hening (ed.), *Statutes*, II, 267. The distinction between white and colored women was neatly described at the turn of the century by Robert Beverley, *The History and Present State of Virginia*, Louis B. Wright, ed. (Chapel Hill, 1947), 271–72.
29. Hening (ed.), *Statutes*, I, 226, and for the same act in more detail see *William and Mary Quarterly*, s. 2, IV (July 1924), 147. The Handlins dis-

Finally, an even more compelling sense of the separateness of Negroes was revealed in early distress concerning sexual union between the races. In 1630 a Virginia court pronounced a now famous sentence: "Hugh Davis to be soundly whipped, before an assembly of Negroes and others for abusing himself to the dishonor of God and shame of Christians, by defiling his body in lying with a negro."[30] While there were other instances of punishment for interracial union in the ensuing years, fornication rather than miscegenation may well have been the primary offense, though in 1651 a Maryland man sued someone who he claimed had said "that he had a black bastard in Virginia."[31] There may have been nothing racial about the 1640 case by which Robert Sweet was compelled "to do penance in church according to laws of England, for getting a negroe woman with child and the woman whipt."[32] About 1650 a white man and a Negro woman were required to stand clad in white sheets before a congregation in Lower Norfolk County for having had relations, but this punishment was sometimes used in ordinary cases of fornication between two whites.[33]

---

counted this law: "Until the 1660's the statutes on the Negroes were not at all unique. Nor did they add up to a decided trend." ("Origins," 209.) The note added to this statement reads, "That there was no trend is evident from the fluctuations in naming Negroes slaves or servants and in their right to bear arms. See Hening, *Statutes*, I, 236, 258, 292, 540; Bruce, *Institutional History*, II, 5 ff., 190 ff. For similar fluctuations with regard to Indians, see Hening, *Statutes*, I, 391, 518." But since the terms "servants" and "slaves" did not have precise meaning, as the Handlins themselves asserted, fluctuations in naming Negroes one or the other can not be taken to mean that their status itself was fluctuating. Of the pages cited in Hening, p. 258 is an act encouraging Dutch traders and contains nothing about Negroes, servants, slaves, or arms. Page 292 is an act providing that fifteen tithable persons should support one soldier; Negroes were among those tithable, but nothing was said of allowing them to arm. Page 540 refers to "any negro slaves" and "said negro," but mentions nothing about servants or arms. In the pages dealing with Indians, p. 391 provides that no one is to employ Indian servants with guns, and p. 518 that Indians (not "Indian servants") are to be allowed to use their own guns; the two provisions are not contradictory. Philip A. Bruce, *Institutional History of Virginia in the Seventeenth Century* (2 vols., New York, 1910), II, 5 ff., indicates that Negroes were barred from arming in 1639 and offers no suggestion that there was any later fluctuation in this practice.

30. Hening (ed.), *Statutes*, I, 146. "Christianity" appears instead of "Christians" in McIlwaine (ed.), *Minutes of the Council*, 479.

31. *Maryland Archives*, X, 114–15.

32. Hening (ed.), *Statutes*, I, 552; McIlwaine, *Minutes of the Council*, 477.

33. Bruce, *Economic History of Virginia*, II, 110.

It is certain, however, that in the early 1660's when slavery was gaining statutory recognition, the colonial assemblies legislated with feeling against miscegenation. Nor was this merely a matter of avoiding confusion of status, as was suggested by the Handlins. In 1662 Virginia declared that "if any christian shall committ ffornication with a negro man or woman, hee or shee soe offending" should pay double the usual fine. Two years later Maryland prohibited interracial marriages:

forasmuch as divers freeborne English women forgettfull of their free Condicōn and to the disgrace of our Nation doe intermarry with Negro Slaves by which alsoe divers suites may arise touching the Issue of such woemen and a great damage doth befall the Masters of such Negros for prevention whereof for deterring such freeborne women from such shamefull Matches...,

strong language indeed if the problem had only been confusion of status. A Maryland act of 1681 described marriages of white women with Negroes as, among other things, "always to the Satisfaccōn of theire Lascivious & Lustfull desires, & to the disgrace not only of the English butt allso of many other Christian Nations." When Virginia finally prohibited all interracial liaisons in 1691, the assembly vigorously denounced miscegenation and its fruits as "that abominable mixture and spurious issue."[34]

34. Hening (ed.), *Statutes*, II, 170; III, 86–87; *Maryland Archives*, I, 533–34; VII, 204. Opinion on this matter apparently was not unanimous, for a petition of several citizens to the Council in 1699 asked repeal of the intermarriage prohibition. H. R. McIlwaine (ed.), *Legislative Journals of the Council of Colonial Virginia* (3 vols., Richmond, 1918–1919), I, 262. The Handlins wrote ("Origins," 215), "Mixed marriages of free men and servants were particularly frowned upon as complicating status and therefore limited by law." Their citation for this, Hening (ed.), *Statutes*, II, 114 (1661/62), and Marcus W. Jernegan, *Laboring and Dependent Classes in Colonial America, 1607–1783* (Chicago, 1931), 55, 180, gives little backing to the statement. In Virginia secret marriage or bastardy between whites of different status got the same punishment as such between whites of the same status. A white servant might marry any white if his master consented. See Hening (ed.), *Statutes*, I, 252–53, 438–39; II, 114–15, 167; III, 71–75, 137–40. See also James C. Ballagh, *White Servitude in the Colony of Virginia* (Baltimore, 1895), 50. For Maryland, see *Maryland Archives*, I, 73, 373–74, 441–42; II, 396-97; XIII, 501–502. The Handlins also suggested that in the 1691 Virginia law, "spurious" meant simply "illegitimate," and they cited Arthur W. Calhoun, *A Social History of the American Family from*

One is confronted, then, with the fact that the first evidences of enslavement and of other forms of debasement appeared at about the same time. Such coincidence comports poorly with both views on the causation of prejudice and slavery. If slavery caused prejudice, then invidious distinctions concerning working in the fields, bearing arms, and sexual union should have appeared only after slavery's firm establishment. If prejudice caused slavery, then one would expect to find such lesser discriminations preceding the greater discrimination of outright enslavement.

Perhaps a third explanation of the relationship between slavery and prejudice may be offered, one that might fit the pattern of events as revealed by existing evidence. Both current views share a common starting point: They predicate two factors, prejudice and slavery, and demand a distinct order of causality. No matter how qualified by recognition that the effect may in turn react upon the cause, each approach inevitably tends to deny the validity of its opposite. But what if one were to regard both slavery and prejudice as species of a general debasement of the Negro? Both may have been equally cause and effect, constantly reacting upon each other, dynamically joining hands to hustle the Negro down the road to complete degradation. Mutual causation is, of course, a highly useful concept for describing social situations in the modern world.[35] Indeed it has been widely applied in only slightly altered fashion to the current racial situation: Racial prejudice and the Negro's lowly position are widely accepted as constantly reinforcing each other.

This way of looking at the facts might well fit better with what we know of slavery itself. Slavery was an organized pattern of human relationships. No matter what the law might say, it was of different character than cattle ownership. No matter how degrading, slavery involved human beings. No one seriously pretended otherwise. Slavery was not an isolated economic or institutional phenomenon; it was the practical facet of a general debasement without which slavery could have no rationality. (Prejudice, too, was a form of debasement,

---

Colonial Times to the Present (3 vols., Cleveland, O., 1917–1919), I, 42, which turns out to be one quotation from John Milton. However, "spurious" was used in colonial laws with reference only to unions between white and black, and never in bastardy laws involving whites only. Mulattoes were often labeled "spurious" offspring.

35. For example, George C. Homans, *The Human Group* (New York, 1950).

a kind of slavery in the mind.) Certainly the urgent need for labor in a virgin country guided the direction which debasement took, molded it, in fact, into an institutional framework. That economic practicalities shaped the external form of debasement should not tempt one to forget, however, that slavery was at bottom a social arrangement, a way of society's ordering its members in its own mind.

William S. Willis,
"Divide and Rule:
Red, White, and Black in the Southeast"

Three races, red, black, and white, resided in the British North
American colonies. In "Divide and Rule," William Willis examines
the relationships among the races in eighteenth-century
South Carolina where a white minority lived among larger black
and red populations. The whites feared both nonwhite majorities
as a threat to their security, and particularly, dreaded a black and red
alliance against their domination. Willis details the means by
which whites attempted to separate and alienate the two
majorities from each other. By making each an accomplice in
the struggle to subjugate the other and by creating hostility
between them, South Carolina whites were able to divide and rule.

Divide and Rule:
Red, White, and Black
in the Southeast

William S. Willis

North of Mexico, the Colonial Southeast was the only place where Indians, Whites, and Negroes met in large numbers.[1] Little of the fascinating story of this contact has been told and some crucial parts may be beyond recall for lack of documents. The early attitude of Indians toward Negroes is obviously of great importance. To some extent, it has been dealt with, but conclusions have differed. Laurence Foster and James Johnston are certain that the early feeling of Indians was one of friendliness.[2] On the other hand, some students, mainly Southern historians, stress hostility.[3] As a matter of fact, a

Abridged from William S. Willis, "Divide and Rule: Red, White, and Black in the Southeast," pp. 157–176. Copyright © by The Association for the Study of Negro Life and History, Inc. Published in *The Journal of Negro History*, XLVIII (July 1963). Some footnotes have been renumbered.

1. Gratitude is extended to Margaret Furcron, Brooklyn College, to Elliott P. Skinner, New York University, and especially to Morton H. Fried, Columbia University, for valuable suggestions, but any infelicities of style or errors of fact are the author's.

2. Laurence Foster, *Negro-Indian Relationships in the Southeast* (Philadelphia, 1935), p. 74; James H. Johnston, "Documentary Evidence of the Relations of Negroes and Indians," *Journal of Negro History*, XIV (January, 1929), pp. 21–23.

3. W. J. Rivers, *A Sketch of the History of South Carolina* (Charleston, 1856), p. 48; W. C. Macleod, *The American Indian Frontier* (New York, 1928), p. 306; Chapman J. Milling, *Red Carolinians* (Chapel Hill, 1940), p. 63.

great deal of hostility seems to have existed in the eighteenth century. In 1752, the Catawba Indians showed great anger and bitter resentment when a Negro came among them as a trader.[4] Perhaps the Cherokee had the strongest color prejudice of all Indians. Even the Spaniards were not "White" enough for them. In 1793, Little Turkey, a prominent chief, declared that Spaniards were not "real white people, and what few I have seen of them looked like mulattoes, and I would never have anything to say to them."[5] According to John Brickell, an early eighteenth century reporter, Indians had a "natural aversion to the Blacks."[6] In 1763, George Milligen Johnston, a South Carolina physician, opined that this hostility was mutual and spoke of the "natural Dislike and Antipathy, that subsists between them [Negroes] and our Indian Neighbors."[7] But the Southern historians have not explained why Indians disliked Negroes. This paper examines this hostility, and that of Negroes to Indians. The story is the familiar one of divide and rule. Specifically, it will be shown that Whites willfully helped create the antagonism between Indians and Negroes in order to preserve themselves and their privileges.

In the Colonial Southeast, Negro slavery and trade with Indians were more prominent in South Carolina than anywhere else. The province sanctioned slavery from its beginnings in 1670, but South Carolinians brought in few Negroes until the late 1690's. From that time, the steady increase in the number of Negro slaves correlates with the steadily increasing demand for labor. First, there was the expansion of rice production on slave-operated plantations. This occurred at about the same time, near the turn of the eighteenth century, that the general supply of slaves in the New World swelled. In the 1720's, the manufacture of pitch and tar, and in the 1740's the growth of indigo production added to the demand for slave labor. Meanwhile other events conspired to curtail other supplies of labor. Indian slavery dwindled and virtually disappeared after the Yamassee War of 1715–1717. This rebellion of tribes trading with the province produced a widespread notion that South Carolina was a dangerous

---

4. W. L. McDowell (ed.), *Documents relating to Indian Affairs, May 21, 1750–August 7, 1754* (Columbia, 1959), p. 201.

5. *American State Papers, Indian Affairs*, I, 461.

6. John Brickell, *The Natural History of North Carolina* (Dublin, 1737), p. 263.

7. Milling (ed.), *Colonial South Carolina: Two Contemporary Descriptions* (Columbia, 1951), p. 136.

place and few Whites entered for two decades after the fighting. The demand for Negroes grew in tandem with the mounting political power of the planters and the government was increasingly responsive to the latter's demands. By the beginning of the eighteenth century, Negroes outnumbered Whites and they increased their proportion of the population later in the century when various estimates put the ratio at two or three to one and even higher.[8]

Despite allegations about the submissiveness of Negroes and their acquiescence to slavery, eighteenth century Whites were afraid of their slaves. This fear grew as Negroes became more numerous. Whites especially dreaded slave insurrections; to South Carolinians, Negro rebels were an "intestine Enemy the most dreadful of Enemies."[9] The eighteenth century was punctuated by a steady succession of insurrectionary plots and actual insurrections. Indeed, the Charles Town government at times kept half of its soldiers in the capital. Negroes also struck back at their masters in other ways. They poisoned them, they set fires, and they committed suicide. They also employed subtle everyday resistances, such as, malingering and feigned stupidity. They also ran away. Some went for only short periods to nearby places; others went permanently to distant hiding places, to the mountains and swamps, to the Indian country, and to the Spanish in Florida. Running south to Florida became especially common after the Yamassee War when Spain encouraged more Negroes to come and offered them freedom. By the late 1720's, Negro subversion had become the main defense problem of South Carolina.[10]

Indians were also a big problem, and they were feared. The Colonial Southeast was an arena of an unremitting struggle for empire among Whites: English, French, Spanish, and later Americans. Indian tribes were caught in the middle of this struggle; and Whites competed for their allegiance, for their trade and their warriors. Suc-

8. David D. Wallace, *South Carolina: A Short History, 1520–1948* (Chapel Hill, 1951), *passim*; Verner W. Crane, *The Southern Frontier, 1670–1732* (Durham, 1928), *passim.*

9. J. H. Easterby (ed.), *Journals of the Commons House of Assembly, September 12, 1739–March 26, 1741* (Columbia, 1952), p. 97.

10. Herbert Aptheker, *American Negro Slave Revolts* (New York, 1943), *passim*; Alexander Garden to Secretary, October 31, 1759, Society for the Propagation of the Gospel in Foreign Parts MSS (later cited as SPG MSS), Series B, II, Pt. 1, 962 Library of Congress; Robert L. Meriwether, *The Expansion of South Carolina, 1729–1765* (Kingsport, 1940), p. 6.

cess in the empire struggle depended upon success in the Indian country. For a decade at least, the mere survival of South Carolina remained uncertain and the position of the province among Indians was precarious. But even before the eighteenth century, South Carolina had become much more secure and had constructed a remarkable system of Indian alliances. These alliances gave South Carolina sway over the majority of Indians in the South and forced the Spanish and French to keep retreating. Through its successes, South Carolina became confident, perhaps overconfident, of controlling Indians. Then came the Yamassee War. For a time South Carolinians were on the verge of being driven into the sea; however, in the end they had their victory. But with all the devastation, their province emerged from the war weakened and insecure, with Spain and France stronger than ever. The old confidence of managing Indians was gone, and gone for good. They now believed more than ever that Indians could never be really trusted. From now on, they and all Whites lived in dread of the next Indian uprising—an uprising that would be supported by enemy Whites.[11]

The picture in the Colonial Southeast was this: a frightened and dominant White minority faced two exploited colored majorities.[12] To meet the Negro danger, South Carolina devised a harsh slave code; the police control of slaves was comprehensive, specific, and brutal. To meet the Indian danger, the province had a system of trade regulation that was less brutal than the slave code but of approximately equal thoroughness. That Indian tribes were still independent and had some freedom of choice necessitated their being dealt with somewhat like equals. After the Yamassee War, the province played tribe off against tribe; indeed, village against village.[13] They also watched the munitions trade to prevent any stockpiling of arms.[14] In meeting each danger, South Carolinians were plagued by

11. Crane, *passim*.

12. Around 1750, Whites were estimated at 30–40,000; Indians, 60,000; Negroes, 70–90,000. Kenneth W. Porter, "Negroes on the Southern Frontier," *Journal of Negro History*, XXXIII (January, 1948), 53–54.

13. Commons House of Assembly to Francis Nicholson, February 3, 1721, Great Britain Public Record Office, Colonial Office (later cited as CO), 5/426, pp. 20–21, Library of Congress.

14. McDowell (ed.), *Journals of the Commissioners of the Indian Trade, September 20, 1710–August 29, 1718* (Columbia, 1955), p. 137.

the discrepancy between what they willed and what they could actually do. This discrepancy became greater with time. It did not take much imagination on the part of Whites to put the two dangers, Indians and Negro slaves, together. As early as 1712, Governor Alexander Spotswood, of Virginia, juxtaposed them.[15] In 1729, the French delayed sending an expedition against the Natchez Indians who had slaughtered French citizens because they feared that New Orleans without troops would be attacked by the Choctaw Indians, and Negroes in order to "free themselves from slavery, might join them."[16] This was the biggest fear of all. In 1775, John Stuart, British Superintendent of Southern Indian Affairs, explained that "nothing can be more alarming to Carolinians than the idea of an attack from Indians and Negroes."[17]

What did South Carolinians do about this nightmare? One answer was, keep Indians and Negroes apart—do not let them mix. In 1757, Captain Daniel Pepper, agent to the Creek Indians, stated that "intimacy" between Indians and Negroes should be avoided.[18] In 1767, Stuart expressed this idea again, perhaps even more strongly: "any Intercourse between Indians and Negroes in my opinion ought to be prevented as much as possible."[19] If this were done, Negroes could not establish personal relations with Indians and learn their languages. This would eliminate the dreaded coordinated blow by Indians and Negroes. But Whites also had other goals in mind. Whites believed that whenever Negro and Indian talked in private the talk was against them. The government believed that Negroes could spread discontent among the tribes and foil its schemes in the Indian country. In 1779, the British Indian Service stated that "Negroes infused many very bad notions into their [Indians] minds."[20] To do this, Negroes need not always lie; as servants, they were some-

15. *Colonial Records of North Carolina*, I, 886.

16. Reuben G. Thwaites (ed.), *Jesuit Relations* (Cleveland, 1900), LIX, 189.

17. *Colonial Records of North Carolina*, X, 118.

18. Pepper to Lyttelton, March 30, 1757, South Carolina Indian Book, February 21, 1757–March 6, 1760, p. 19, Library of Congress.

19. Stuart to Gage, November 27, 1767, Thomas Gage Papers, William L. Clements Library, Ann Arbor.

20. Report of Board of Commissioners, August 16, 1779, CO, 5/81, p. 451.

times privy to important secrets. Moreover, the government was double-dealing with its Indian allies; for instance, stirring up trouble between Creeks and Cherokee. On the other hand, Indians could offer freedom to Negroes and tell them how to get to their villages.

To this end of keeping these colored peoples apart, South Carolinians tried to prevent Indians from coming into the province unless they were on official business. In 1742, a Committee on Indian Affairs warned against frequent visiting by Indians because of the hazard of their associating with slaves, "particularly in regard to their talking, and having too great Intercourse with our Slaves, at the out-plantations, where they camp."[21] Even when on official missions to Charles Town, chiefs were discouraged from bringing too many *aides-de-camp* and were hurried away as quickly as possible.[22] The Settlement Indians, those partially detribalized natives living within the province, presented a special problem. Here again the government opposed contact with Negroes; trading and intermarriage were frowned upon.[23] This determination to prevent Indian-Negro contacts within the White settlements was a main cause for curtailing the enslavement of Indians. Indian slaves got to know Negroes and, since they escaped easily into the hinterland, they might carry Negroes along with them. In 1729, Governor Etienne Perier, of Louisiana, explained that "Indian slaves being mixed with our negroes may induce them to desert."[24]

Keeping Negroes and Indians apart had another aim: keep Negroes out of the Indian country. Eighteenth century legislation consistently prohibited any Negro, slave or free, from going to any Indian tribe either as a trader in his own right or as a White trader's helper.[25] Violations of this prohibition almost always led to hasty action to

---

21. Report of Committee on Indian Affairs, May 27, 1742, CO, 5/443, p. 31.

22. McDowell, *Documents*, p. 109.

23. Report of Committee on Indian Affairs, February 29, 1727, CO, 5/430, p. 37.

24. Dunbar Rowland and A. G. Sanders (eds.), *Mississippi Provincial Archives, French Dominion, 1701–1729* (Jackson, 1929), I, 573. Later cited as *MPAFD*.

25. Crane, p. 203; John R. Alden, *John Stuart and the Southern Colonial Frontier, 1754–1775* (Ann Arbor, 1944), pp. 19, 342.

remove these Negroes. Later in the eighteenth century when the westward movement was getting into high gear, opposition to Whites taking their slaves into Indian country became an important obstruction to White settlement of the interior.[26]

Fugitive Negroes among the Indians were the biggest headache. In 1767, Stuart declared that "to prevent the Indian Country [from] becoming an Asylum for Negroes is a Matter of the Utmost consequence to the prosperity of the provinces."[27] To keep slaves from escaping, South Carolina assigned patrols to watch the roads and countryside; to keep Indian raiding parties out of the province, the government built forts at key approaches and sent rangers out to ride along the frontiers. But Indians were excellent slave catchers. The Settlement Indians in particular were regularly employed to track down fugitive slaves; indeed, slave catching was so profitable to them that they readily agreed in 1727 to move their villages so that they could do a better job.[28] . . .

Keeping Negroes and Indians apart had still another aim: keep Negroes out of the swamps and the mountains. Negroes frequently escaped to these out of the way places. These fugitives, called Maroons, preferred the swamps, especially those in the direction of St. Augustine. . . .

Maroons were the most resourceful of all fugitives. They aimed at nothing less than setting up small self-sufficient societies in the most inhospitable places. They had to plan ahead, carefully and secretly. They knew a hard life of hard work and hard fighting awaited them. [For example], fifteen Virginia Maroons carried guns, ammunition, clothing, furniture, and implements into the mountains; before they were captured, they had started clearing land in order to farm. Once established in their fastnesses, Maroons then lived as banditti; they plundered White settlements, killing masters and rescuing slaves. In 1717, a band under the leadership of one Sebastian terrorized the southern parishes of South Carolina.[29] In the early 1770's, a frightened William Bartram, the noted naturalist, encountered a band of

---

26. Stuart to Gage, March 19, 1765 and December 27, 1767, Gage Papers.

27. Stuart to Gage, September 26, 1767, op. cit.

28. Report of Committee on Indian Affairs, February 29, 1727, CO, 5/430, p. 37.

29. Wallace, *The History of South Carolina* (New York, 1934), I, 372.

marauders north of Charles Town and later explained that "people were ... frequently attacked, robbed, and sometimes murdered" by Negro bands in this region.[30] These Maroons were dangerous men and women, and they struck out against slavery. No threat, however, was greater than the possibility of their cooperating with hostile Indians and coordinating their attacks against White settlements. Top priority was given by Whites to the immediate destruction of the Maroons. This job was too important to be handled by a local community. Instead the government sent soldiers into the wilderness to eliminate them.[31] Indians were also called upon to help, and they were especially good at ferreting out Maroons from their lurking places.[32]

In addition to keeping Indians and Negroes apart, Whites pitted the colored groups against each other. In 1725, Richard Ludlam, a South Carolina minister, confessed that "we make use of a Wile for our prest. Security to make Indians & Negro's a checque upon each other least by their Vastly Superior Numbers we should be crushed by one or the other."[33] How did Whites go about this? The essential thing was to make bad blood between them: create suspicion, fear, and hatred. In 1758, James Glen, long governor of South Carolina, explained to William Lyttelton, his inexperienced successor, that "it has been allways the policy of this govert to creat an aversion in them [Indians] to Negroes."[34] ...

Whites sought to convince Indians that Negroes worked against their best interests. In October, 1715, the Cherokee were on the verge of deserting their Indian confederates in the Yamassee War and joining South Carolina in an attack upon the Creeks. They hoped for a better trade with Charles Town and more security in the South. However, two runaway Negroes from South Carolina came to the Cherokee villages and, according to the South Carolinians, told these Indians a "parcell of lies" which dissuaded the Cherokee from joining

30. Mark Van Doren (ed.), *The Travels of William Bartram* (New York, 1940), p. 371.

31. Peter Timothy to Lyttelton, November 13, 1759, Lyttelton Papers.

32. E. Merton Coulter (ed.), *The Journal of William Stephens, 1743–1745* (Athens, 1959), II, 245.

33. Ludlam to Secretary, March, 1725, SPG MSS, A, 19, p. 85.

34. Glen to Lyttelton, January 23, 1758, Lyttelton Papers.

the South Carolinians.[35] Later in January, 1716, the Cherokee finally went over to the province; on their part, the South Carolinians agreed to specific commitments for a larger trade at cheap prices and for military support against all enemies of the Cherokee. For a while, it seemed that the province really intended to live up to these commitments and the Cherokee were happy with their new friends in Charles Town.[36] During this time, Whites lost no chance of reminding the Indians that Negroes had almost prevented this boon from coming their way. . . .

Whites also contributed to this aversion by using Negro slaves as soldiers against Indians. These slaves were rewarded with goods and sometimes with their freedom. Negroes made good soldiers against other Negroes in rebellion; if they did this against their own people, they certainly had no compunction about fighting Indians.[37] In the Yamassee War, trusted Negroes were drafted and armed and then sent against enemy Indians in the province. Later they were also used against enemy Indians in the interior. . . .

Employing Indians as slave catchers encouraged anti-Negro sentiment among the Indians themselves. Whites paid Indians well for returning fugitive slaves; for instance, at the great Augusta Conference in 1763, the price was set at one musket and three blankets for each slave brought in. The Indian trade was largely based on deerskins, and these skins were sold cheaply to the traders; in order to buy a musket and three blankets, an Indian had to pay about thirty-five skins. This required several months of hunting.[38] Moreover, the hunting grounds were dangerous places; enemies were always lurking about. Hence, an Indian often lost time fighting, if he were lucky enough not to lose his life. In a word, Indians were usually short of goods and in debt. The reward for fugitive slaves was, therefore, something they could rarely afford to turn down. Moreover, the avariciousness of Indians was proverbial in the South.[39]

35. Langdon Cheves (ed.), "Journal of the March of the Carolinians into the Cherokee Mountains, 1715–1716," *Year Book of the City of Charleston for 1894*, p. 344.

36. Crane, pp. 180–184, 193–194.

37. Easterby, p. 64.

38. Stuart to Gage, August 31, 1771, Gage Papers.

39. McDowell, *Documents, passim*.

But Indians knew what slavery was like among Whites. They saw its cruelty and brutality whenever they visited the White settlements. They also remembered that Whites had once enslaved Indians in large numbers and occasionally still did so. Indeed, the great fear of Indians was that Whites, and especially South Carolinians, would at some time make slaves of all Indians in the South. This fear was in the background of all their dealings with Whites.[40] All of this worked in two contradictory ways on Indians. Self-interest made the Indian act as an enemy of Negro freedom; but human feelings made him guilty. Like other men in this ambivalence, he suppressed his guilt with a convenient hostility.

Since it was important that Negroes should fear and hate Indians, it is likely that Whites told their slaves many horror stories about Indians, especially those depicting the terrible things that Indians did to Negroes. Actually it was not difficult to portray Indians in a bad light. Indians did kill and they were cruel. Sometimes their raiding parties striking swiftly and with surprise killed Negroes alongside their White masters.[41] Indians also scalped and otherwise mutilated their victims regardless of race.[42] Besides, Indians were known in the early days to subject their male captives to prolonged and deadly tortures; now and then they did this even in the eighteenth century. . . . But atrocities were not the main thing. The main thing was that Indians often behaved as real enemies of Negro freedom. To a large extent, Whites encouraged Indians to act this way. As we shall see, this was partly done to make Negroes fear and hate Indians. Given this aim, we assume that Whites publicized these unfriendly acts of Indians among their slaves—and conveniently overlooked their own responsibility . We will now give attention to some situations in which Indians behaved as enemies of Negro freedom.

As we know, Whites employed Indians as slave catchers, and Indians were eager for these jobs. Moreover, Negroes knew that Indians, being expert woodsmen, were better slave catchers than White soldiers and patrols.[43] Negroes also realized that death sometimes

40. Edmund Atkin to Lyttelton, November 3, 1759, Lyttelton Papers.

41. George Gilmer, *Sketches of Some of the First Settlers of Upper Georgia* (Americus, 1926), p. 251.

42. *American State Papers, Indian Affairs*, I, 452.

43. Glen to Newcastle, April 14, 1748, CO, 5/389, p. 58.

awaited the unsuccessful runaway instead of a return to slavery. The
Charles Town government executed leaders of fugitive slave parties
and those slaves who ran away repeatedly. This government also instructed slave catchers to kill fugitive Negroes when they could not
capture them; therefore, dead fugitives were paid for as well as live
ones.[44] This encouraged Indians to be more bloodthirsty than White
slave catchers: the labor of these fugitives was not going to benefit
them. Besides, scalping was more profitable to them than to Whites:
Indians could make one scalp look like two or more scalps. To prevent this cheating, the Charles Town government tried to buy only
scalps with two ears.[45] . . .

Indians were *bona fide* slave traders. They stole Negroes from
White slaveholders in order to sell them to other White slaveholders.
Indians had been prepared for this Negro trade by the earlier trade
in Indian slaves; for instance, they had learned that male captives
were often too valuable to be done away with. Except for raids by
Spanish Indians against South Carolina, Indians did not steal too
many Negroes in the first half of the eighteenth century. About the
only other Indians that regularly raided for Negro slaves were the
Chickasaw and other allied tribes of South Carolina living near the
Mississippi River. These tribes raided French settlements in Louisiana
and French convoys on the Great River. Negroes captured in these
raids were sold to Charles Town traders who carried them to South
Carolina.[46] This trade did not bring many slaves into the province;
the French were always so short of Negroes. For the Negroes, this
trade was a calamity. Their capture meant the substitution of one
enslavement by a more severe one. Therefore, these Negroes must
have been bitter anti-Indian propagandists among the slaves of South
Carolina. . . .

Finally, Whites employed Indians to help crush slave insurrections.
In the Stono Rebellion of 1739, the most serious insurrection in
South Carolina during the eighteenth century, about eighty Negro
slaves killed more than thirty Whites. At the outset, the Charles
Town government called upon Settlement Indians for help. These

44. Aptheker, "Maroons within the Present Limits of the United States," *Journal
of Negro History*, XXIV (April, 1939), 169.

45. Samuel Hazard (ed.), *Pennsylvania Archives*, 1756–1760 (Philadelphia,
1853), III, 200; Easterby, p. 681.

46. *MPAFD*, III, 635.

Indians pursued those slaves who eluded the militia at Stono; in a few weeks, they managed to capture some of these slaves and to kill a few others.[47] Indians also aided the province in suppressing slave insurrections in 1744 and 1765.[48] Slave insurrections in the eighteenth century were small-scale affairs; South Carolinians did not need many Indians to help them restore order in any particular one. What mattered most was speed in putting them down; otherwise, more timid Negroes might respond to the call of liberty and join the rebel slaves. Therefore, for this job, the Charles Town government turned to Settlement Indians and Eastern Siouans. Although few in numbers, these Indians lived closer to White settlements and could be quickly mustered whenever needed.

The Charles Town government paid Indians high wages for helping suppress slave insurrections. In the Stono Rebellion, each Indian was given a coat, a flap, a pair of stockings, a hat, a gun, two pounds of powder, and eight pounds of bullets. The legislature, dominated by large slaveholders whose eyes were on the future, wanted to increase this payment. It declared that "Indians should be encouraged in such manner as to induce them always to offer their Service whenever this Government may have Occasion for them."[49] In 1744, the Natchez, now living as scattered Settlement Indians in South Carolina after their defeat by the French in 1729, informed Governor Glen that they wanted to be "together to be ready to assist the Government in case of any Insurrection, or Rebellion of the Negroes."[50] We can be certain that Negroes knew how eager Indians were to help keep them in slavery.

The Charles Town government did not wait for an uprising before calling on Indians. This government tried to anticipate trouble and then prevent it by using Indians to intimidate Negroes. On November 10, 1739, less than two months after Stono, the legislature ordered its Committee on Indian Affairs to cooperate with its special committee investigating this insurrection in "finding the most effectual

---

47. Easterby, *passim.*
48. Milling, *Red Carolinians*, p. 229; Wallace, *South Carolina: Short History,* p. 185.
49. Easterby, pp. 65, 76–77.
50. South Carolina Council Journal, December 11, 1743–December 8, 1744, CO, 5/448, pp. 187–188.

means for preventing of such Dangers throughout the province." South Carolinians feared insurrections especially at Christmas, Negroes having so much more free time during these holidays.[51] During the Christmas of 1716, the Charles Town government ordered Settlement Indians to move nearer White settlements to terrorize the slaves. Moreover, the government made a practice of locating Settlement Indians near places at which slaves might become troublesome. In the summer of 1716, it maintained the Wineau Indians around the Santee settlements "for keeping ye Negroes in awe."[52] But South Carolinians did not rely only on Settlement Indians to prevent insurrections. These tribes and even the Catawba were not large enough to intimidate all Negroes in the province; there were not enough Settlement Indians to station at every danger point. As we know, South Carolinians saw the danger of a big insurrection in every little one. For intimidating all slaves, South Carolina needed at least one big inland tribe. Therefore, the government turned to its most trusted ally and probably the tribe most hostile to Negroes: the Cherokee. In 1737, Lieutenant-Governor Thomas Broughton reported that he was sending for Cherokee warriors "to come down to the settlements to be an awe to the negroes."[53] Thus, a special effort was made after the Yamassee War to keep Negroes isolated from the Cherokee. In 1741, the legislature requested that Broughton purchase two Negro slaves owned by a Cherokee chief so that they could be shipped to the "West Indies or Northern Colonies to prevent any Detriment that they might do this Province by getting acquainted with the Cherokees."[54] It is clear that this intimidation by Indians helped prevent slave insurrections.

Conclusion

Hostility between Indians and Negroes in the Colonial Southeast was more pronounced than friendliness. Southern Whites were afraid of these two colored races, each of which outnumbered them. Whites

---

51. Easterby, pp. 24, 69.
52. Wallace, *History of South Carolina*, I, 185; McDowell, *Journals*, p. 80.
53. Quoted in Wallace, *History of South Carolina*, I, 368.
54. Easterby (ed.), *Journals of the Commons House of Assembly, May 18, 1741–July 10, 1742* (Columbia, 1953), p. 45.

were especially afraid that these two exploited races would combine against them. To prevent this combination, Whites deliberately maintained social distance between Indians and Negroes and created antagonism between them. To maintain this social distance, Whites segregated Indians and Negroes from each other. They did this by keeping Indians out of White settlements as much as possible and by trying to keep Negroes out of the Indian country and other out of the way places where these colored races might meet. To create antagonism, Whites deliberately played Indians and Negroes against each other. They pointed out to these races that each was the enemy of the other. To this end of mutual hostility, Whites also used Negroes as soldiers against Indians; on the other hand, they used Indians to catch runaway slaves and to suppress slave insurrections. In the eyes of Negroes, Indians were enemies of Negro freedom. At times, Whites encouraged Indians and Negroes to murder each other. In these ways, Whites created much of the hostility between Indians and Negroes in the eighteenth century.

Part III
Revolutionary Ideals and Minority Realities, 1763-1842

Revolutionary Ideals and Minority Realities, 1763–1842

In the eight decades between 1763 and 1842, the United States fought a successful war for independence and established a republican government based on the idealistic rhetoric of the American Revolution. American revolutionary ideals, articulated by Thomas Jefferson in the Declaration of Independence, indicated a commitment to the concept "that all men are created equal, that they are endowed by their Creator with certain unalienable Rights, that among these are Life, liberty and the pursuit of Happiness." The history of the nation in the decades following 1776 reveals a steady growth of democracy as a national ideal and reality. The reality, however, was limited to whites because neither blacks nor Indians shared in the "blessings of liberty" secured by the American Revolution.

Most of the Indians in British North America at the beginning of the revolution lived west of the Allegheny Mountains, where the British government attempted to protect them from further incursions by white settlers. The policy of deterring white expansion beyond the Alleghenies irritated many colonists, and some land-hungry whites viewed the break with England as a means of securing new properties. As a result most Indians were hostile to the American cause, and many, like those who fought under the Mohawk warrior, Joseph Brant, actively supported the British. The victory of the colonials opened the West to white settlement. Some Indian lands between the Alleghenies and the Mississippi River were taken by conquest and some by purchase, but the American government never deviated from its policy of populating the new territory with white farmers.

The United States government pursued the different and often conflicting approaches of "civilization" and removal in its dealings with the Indians. "Civilization" involved persuading the Indians to abandon hunting for agriculture and to forsake communal ownership of property. Its proponents reasoned that independent Indian farmers would require less land and be more pliable than roving bands of hunters. Removal was a scheme to dispossess the eastern tribes and resettle them west of the Mississippi. Even those nations which adopted "civilization" were not exempt from removal, and by 1850 approximately one hundred thousand Indians had been relocated. The process, accomplished by a combination of force, threats, tricks, and bribes, took a heavy toll in Indian lives and culture.

As did the Indians, many blacks found themselves participants in, but not beneficiaries of, the American Revolution. Both the British and colonial armies used black troops during the revolution, and in some cases slaves were rewarded with freedom for their service. However, revolutionary rhetoric about freedom had little impact on the institution of slavery. The obvious disparity between revolutionary ideals and the reality of slavery caused many whites, including slaveholders, to question the morality of black bondage. The states north of Maryland abolished slavery in the years following the revolution, but in the South discussion of the economic and moral evils of slavery led only to occasional voluntary manumission.

The debates over slavery during the revolutionary period reveal clearly the manner in which slavery and racism were linked in the minds of white Americans. Many whites argued that, although slavery was evil, abolition would be socially disastrous. A society composed of blacks and whites on an equal footing was unthinkable because of the inferiority of blacks. Such notions led to the popularity of colonization schemes with the goal of freeing blacks and relocating them in Africa or elsewhere beyond the borders of the country. Unrealistic as a means of ending slavery, the chimera of colonization beckoned those who wanted to make the United States a white man's nation.

Abolitionists, beginning in the 1830s, directly attacked the institution of slavery by demanding immediate and unequivocal emancipation. The resistance of the slaves themselves, most dramatically in the form of open revolts, constituted a further challenge to the "peculiar institution." Events such as the slave uprising under Gabriel Prosser near Richmond, Virginia (1800), the conspiracy of Denmark Vesey in Charleston, South Carolina (1822), and Nat Turner's rebellion in Southampton County, Virginia (1831) frightened white southerners. Ironically, the attacks of the abolitionists and the slave revolts stiffened the resolve of southern slaveholders to defend and protect slavery, a process which resulted in an even more repressive institution.

White Americans made significant strides toward the democratic government and equalitarian society seemingly promised by the American Revolution. Yet, the growth and prosperity of the nation was accomplished at the expense of the lives and liberties of the two nonwhite minorities which lived within its borders. Blacks and Indians remained the exploited subjects of a nation which believed in democracy for whites only.

Benjamin Quarles,
"Lord Dunmore As Liberator"

Personal liberty as an avowed aim of the American Revolution stood in direct conflict with the possession of slaves. The obvious disparity between principle and practice led many white American revolutionaries to question the practice of slavery. The war itself also had an unsettling effect on slavery as both sides attempted to recruit black soldiers with promises of freedom. In "Lord Dunmore As Liberator," Benjamin Quarles recounts the efforts of the last royal governor of Virginia to raise a black army by urging slaves of revolutionaries to desert their masters. Virginia slaves welcomed Dunmore's offer of freedom, and almost eight hundred joined him despite considerable obstacles. Yet, like so many proposals which promised an end to slavery during this period, Dunmore's scheme ended in disaster. The American Revolution failed to accord its benefits to the enslaved Americans.

Lord Dunmore As Liberator

Benjamin Quarles

In American patriotic tradition the first full-fledged villain to step from the wings as the Revolutionary War unfolded was John Murray, Earl of Dunmore. Like other royal governors in office as the crisis reached its pitch, the Crown's representative in Virginia would have been a marked man no matter how circumspect his behavior. Dunmore, lacking in diplomatic skills, was destined to furnish the colonists with a convenient hate-symbol. The one act that most thoroughly defamed his name was a deed which in Negro circles cast its author in the role of liberator. This was Dunmore's proclamation inviting slaves to leave their masters and join the royal forces.

Issued as of November 7, 1775, on board the *William* in the harbor at Norfolk, the proclamation announced that in order to defeat "treasonable purposes" the governor was establishing martial law. Colonists who refused "to resort to his Majesty's standard" were to be adjudged traitors. Then came the words which were destined to be quoted far and wide: "and I do hereby further declare all indented servants, Negroes, or others, (appertaining to Rebels,) free, that are able and willing to bear arms, they joining His Majesty's Troops, as

Abridged from Benjamin Quarles, "Lord Dunmore As Liberator," *William and Mary Quarterly*, XV (1958), pp. 494–507. Reprinted by permission. Footnotes have been renumbered.

soon as may be, for the more speedily reducing the Colony to a proper sense of their duty, to His Majesty's crown and dignity."[1]

Dunmore's proclamation had its expected effect. "The colonists," wrote a contemporary, "were struck with horror";[2] the "Poet of the American Revolution" implored the heavens to deliver the colonies from the "valiant" Dunmore and "his crew of banditti" ("who plunder Virginians at Williamsburg city").[3] Taking alarm, the Continental Congress lost no time in bestirring itself. On December 2, 1775, the delegates instructed the "Committee for fitting our armed vessels" to engage ships of war for the taking or destroying of the governor's fleet,[4] and the presiding officer urged the commander in chief of the Continental Army to take such measures against his lordship as would "effectually Repel his violences and secure the peace and safety of that Colony."[5] Two days later the Congress recom-

1. Original broadside, 11 by 17 inches, in University of Virginia library. For a facsimile which Patrick Henry circulated, and which differs a little in punctuation from the original, see Francis L. Berkeley, Jr., *Dunmore's Proclamation of Emancipation* (Charlottesville, 1941), frontispiece. See also *American Archives,* comp. Peter Force, 4th Ser. (Washington, 1837–46), III, 1385.

2. David Ramsay, *History of the American Revolution* (Philadelphia, 1789), I, 234.

3. *The Poems of Philip Freneau,* ed. Fred Lewis Pattee (Princeton, 1902–07), I, 140. "Hell itself could not have vomitted anything more black than his design of emancipating our slaves," wrote a Philadelphia correspondent to a friend abroad. *Morning Chronicle and London Advertiser,* Jan. 20, 1776, quoted in *Letters on the American Revolution, 1774–1776,* ed. Margaret W. Willard (Boston, 1925), p. 233. It was the judgment of Edward Rutledge that the proclamation tended "more effectually to work an eternal separation between Great Britain and the Colonies,—than any other expedient, which could possibly have been thought of." Rutledge to Ralph Izard, Dec. 8, 1775, in *Correspondence of Mr. Ralph Izard* (New York, 1844), I, 165.

4. *Journal of the Continental Congress, 1774–1789,* ed. Worthington C. Ford and others (Washington, 1904–37), III, 395.

5. John Hancock to George Washington, Dec. 2, 1775, in *Letters of Members of the Continental Congress,* ed. Edmund C. Burnett (Washington, 1921–36), I, 267. The army commander shared the apprehension of Congress. "If," he wrote to a Virginia delegate, "that man is not crushed before spring, he will become the most formidable enemy America has; his strength will increase as a snow ball by rolling; and faster, if some expedient cannot be hit upon, to convince the slaves and servants of the impotency of his designs." George Washington to Richard Henry Lee, Dec. 26, 1775, in R. H. Lee, *Memoir of the Life of Richard Henry Lee* (Philadelphia, 1825), II, 9. Compare Washington to Joseph Reed, Dec. 15, 1775, in *The Writings of George Washington from the Original Manuscript Sources, 1745–1799,* ed. John C. Fitzpatrick (Washington, 1931–44), IV, 167.

mended to Virginia that she resist Dunmore "to the utmost...."[6]

The apprehension over Dunmore's proclamation was grounded primarily in the fear of its unsettling effect on the slaves, if not in the fear of a servile insurrection—that nightmarish dread in communities where the whites were outnumbered. A policy that would strike off their shackles would obviously have a marked appeal to the inhabitants of slave row. Moreover, there had been recent evidence that the Virginia bondmen were responsive to the offer of freedom.

Dunmore himself had furnished such evidence. For at least eight months prior to the formal proclamation, the governor had seriously considered the idea of enlisting the slaves. His reasons were plain. Rebellious planters who contemplated a resort to arms would be deprived of their workers and would be compelled to return to their homes to protect their families and their property. Moreover, the slaves would help fill the ranks of military laborers for His Majesty's forces, and such human *potentiel de guerre* was badly needed. And Dunmore could expect little help from British headquarters in Boston.[7] Obviously, too, the Crown supporters and their sympathizers counted on the disaffection of the Negroes in the South.[8]

Needing supporters to hold the rebellion-bent Virginians in check, Dunmore let it be known late in April 1775 that he might be driven to set up the royal standard, adding that if he did he believed that

6. *Journals of the Continental Congress*, III, 403.

7. General Thomas Gage wrote to Dunmore on Sept. 10, 1775: "I can neither assist you with Men, arms or ammunition, for I have them not to spare; should you draw upon me I have not the Cash to pay your Bills." Clinton Papers, William L. Clements Library, University of Michigan. For England's continuing great difficulty in getting man power see Edward E. Curtis, *The Organization of the British Army in the American Revolution* (New Haven, 1926), pp. 51–80.

8. "Although Virginia and Maryland are both very populous," wrote Governor Josiah Martin of North Carolina to Dartmouth on June 30, 1775, "the Whites are greatly outnumbered by the Negroes, at least in the former; a circumstance that would facilitate exceedingly the Reduction of those Colonies who are very sensible of their Weakness arising from it." Clinton Papers. This idea of Negro support was a persistent one: "The Negroes may be all deemed so many Intestine Enemies, being all slaves and desirous of Freedom." Joseph Galloway to Dartmouth, Jan. 23, 1778, *Facsimiles of Manuscripts in European Archives Relating to America, 1773–1783*, ed. Benjamin F. Stevens (London, 1889–98), XXIV, no. 2079. For a similar expression from another loyalist, see "Moses Kirkland to His Majesty's Commissioners, Oct. 21, 1778," Clinton Papers.

he could count on "all the Slaves on the side of Government."[9] On May 1 the governor wrote to the Earl of Dartmouth expressing confidence that, once supplied with arms and ammunition, he would be able "to collect from among the Indians,[10] negroes and other persons" a force sufficient to hold his own.[11] Two weeks later, Gage in a letter to Dartmouth touched on Dunmore's proposal: "We hear," wrote the British commander, "that a Declaration his Lordship has made, of proclaiming all the Negroes free, who should join him, has Startled the Insurgents."[12]

In late April a group of slaves, scenting freedom in the air, went to the governor's house and volunteered their services, but Dunmore had them dismissed.[13] He was then not quite ready for the open break, but it would not be long delayed. On June 8, 1775, the governor took the decisive step of quitting Williamsburg and taking asylum aboard the man-of-war Fowey at Yorktown, a move he had been turning over in his mind since May 15.[14] "I have thought it best for his Majesty's service," he wrote, "to retire from amidst such hostile appearances around me."[15] The House of Burgesses, taking note of the governor's flight, assured him that his personal safety was in no danger, but pointedly noted its displeasure that "a Scheme, the most diabolical, had been mediated, and generally recommended,

9. "Deposition of Dr. William Pasteur. In Regard to the Removal of Powder from the Williamsburg Magazine," in "Virginia Legislative Papers (from Originals in Virginia State Archives)," Virginia Magazine of History and Biography, XIII (July 1905), p. 49.
10. Later that year Dunmore concocted a plan to raise the tribes, as Gage phrased it, "on the back Parts of the Province of Virginia, to be Joined by such Inhabitants and Indians as may be at, and about Detroit." Gage to Guy Carleton, Sept. 11, 1775, Gage MSS. (American Series), Clements Library. This so-called "Connolly Plot" is briefly described in Isaac S. Harrell, Loyalism in Virginia (Philadelphia, 1926), pp. 35–37.
11. Dartmouth to Dunmore, Aug. 2, 1775, Amer. Arch., 4th Serv., III, 6. In this passage Dartmouth reports the contents of a letter from Dunmore dated May 1.
12. Gage to Dartmouth, May 15, 1775, Gage MSS. (English Series), Clements Library.
13. "Deposition of John Randolph in Regard to the Removal of the Powder," in "Virginia Legislative Papers," Va. Mag. of His. and Biog., XV (Oct. 1907), 150.
14. Dunmore to Gage, May 15, 1775, Gage MSS. (American Series).
15. Ibid., June 17, 1775.

by a Person of great Influence, to offer Freedom to our Slaves, and turn them against their Masters."[16]

Realizing that there was no turning back, Dunmore initiated a policy of unofficial slave solicitation to augment his tiny force of three hundred white soldiers, seamen, and loyalist recruits. In early August the "Officers of the Volunteer Companies" in Williamsburg informed the Convention that the "Governour's Cutter had carried off a number of Slaves belonging to private gentlemen...."[17] Small sloops, which were employed primarily to intercept intracolonial shipments of powder, invited slaves aboard. "Lord Dunmore sails up and down the river," wrote a Norfolk correspondent on October 28, 1775, to a friend in England, "and where he finds a defenceless place, he lands, plunders the plantation and carries off the negroes."[18]

Now ready to come out into the open, Dunmore was concerned only with his timing. An apparently auspicious moment came in mid-November 1775 when a skirmish took place at Kemp's Landing on the Elizabeth River. In this action the colonial militia was routed and its two commanding colonels were captured. Entering the village in triumph, Dunmore, on November 14, ordered the publication of the proclamation he had drafted a week earlier on board the *William*. The final break had come—the governor had set up his standard and had officially called upon the slaves to join him.

Tidewater Virginia took alarm as rumors spread that the slaves were stampeding to the British.[19] But there were strong deterring factors. Foremost among these was the military alertness of the Virginians themselves. Before any substantial slave migration to Dunmore could get under way the governor suffered a decisive defeat at arms. . . .

16. *Journals of the House of Burgesses of Virginia, 1773–1776*, ed. John Pendleton Kennedy (Richmond, 1905), p. 256.

17. "Proceedings of the Virginia Convention, August 3, 1775," *Amer. Arch.*, 4th Ser., III, 373.

18. *Morning Chronicle and London Advertiser*, Dec. 22, 1775, in Willard, *Letters in the American Revolution*, pp. 271–272. The number of slaves reaching Dunmore during the preproclamation stage is indeterminate; "some accounts make them about 100; others less." Edmund Pendleton and others to Virginia Delegates in Congress, Nov. 11, 1775, Lee Family MSS., U. Va. library.

19. "Letters mention that slaves flock to him in abundance, but I hope it is magnified." Edmund Pendleton to Richard Henry Lee, Nov. 27, 1775, *Amer. Arch.*, 4th Ser., IV, 202.

The military preparation of the colonists was matched by their promptness in adopting "home front" measures to prevent slaves from joining the governor. Newspapers lost no time in publishing the proclamation in full, as information and as a warning. To deter runaways local patrol groups were doubled, highways were carefully watched, and owners of small craft were required to exercise vigilance. Since Dunmore's action had come as no surprise, the Virginians had had time to put the colony in a "tolerable state of defense."[20] Adjacent Maryland, through its Council of Safety, ordered the military to station itself in St. Mary's County "and guard the shores from thence to the river Powtowmack, to prevent any servants, negroes, or others from going on board the Fowey ship of war."[21]

To vigilance the colonists added psychological warfare. In Alexander Purdie's *Virginia Gazette* was published a letter from a subscriber urging that Negroes be cautioned against joining Dunmore. Slaves should be told that the English ministry, in refusing to stop the slave trade, had proved a far greater enemy to Negroes than their American masters, and that if the colonists were defeated, their slaves would be sold to the West Indies. They should be told, too, continued Mr. Purdie's correspondent, that Dunmore was cruel to his own black servitors. And, finally, they should be urged to place their expectation on "a better condition in the next world." If this information had been spread widely, "not one slave would have joined our enemies."[22] ...

Official action was not long in coming. The Virginia Convention on December 8 appointed a committee to prepare an answer to Dunmore's proclamation. Five days later, when the committee made its report, it was directed to draw up a declaration stating that runaways to the British would be pardoned if they returned in ten days; otherwise they would "be liable to such punishment as shall be directed by the Convention." The following day, with the committee's report at hand, the delegates issued a declaration of policy. Beginning with a reminder that the time-honored penalty for a slave insurrection was

20. Ramsay, *American Revolution*, I, 234.

21. *Journal and Correspondence of the Maryland Council of Safety, Aug. 29, 1775–July 6, 1776*, ed. William H. Browne and others, *Archives of Maryland* (Baltimore, 1883—in progress), XI, 511–512.

22. Purdie's *Virginia Gazette*, Williamsburg, Nov. 17, 1775. Hereafter cited as Va. Gaz.

death without benefit of clergy, the document stated that Negroes who had been "seduced" to take up arms were liable to punishment. But in order that they might return in safety to their duties, they would be pardoned if they laid down their arms forthwith. The proclamation concluded with a request to "all humane and benevolent persons in the colony" to convey to the slaves this "offer of mercy."[23] To insure a wide circulation, the proclamation was published as a broadside.[24]

The Virginians supplemented techniques of persuasion and sweet reasonableness with alternatives more forthright and punitive. In early December the Convention decreed that slaves taken in arms were to be sold to the foreign West Indies, with the sale money, minus expenses, to go to their masters.[25] Somewhat less severe was the fate of captured runaways who had failed in their attempts to reach the King's forces. Such slaves, if their masters were patriots, were returned to their home plantations, often after first serving a term of imprisonment. An owner of a captured runaway might be ordered to "convey him to some interior part of the Country as soon as may be. . . ."[26] Slaves of British sympathizers were put to work in the lead mines,[27] a practice which became customary in Virginia for the duration of the war. Distrusting all Negroes who had joined the governor, the Convention recommended that military officers "seize and secure" even those who came bearing flags of truce.[28]

The death penalty was used sparingly. In Northampton County the court passed such a sentence on a group of thirteen slaves who

23. Proceedings of the Convention of the Delegates in the Colony of Virginia (Richmond, 1816), p. 62.

24. Virginia Broadsides (V. 54), U. Va. library.

25. William Waller Hening, The Statutes at Large; Being a Collection of All the Laws of Virginia . . . (Richmond, 1809–23), IX, 106.

26. Such was the language used by the Virginia Council to William Kirby (July 12, 1776) concerning his slave Frank. Journals of the Council of State of Virginia, ed. H. R. McIlwaine and Wilmer L. Hall (Richmond, 1931–32, 1952), I, 67.

27. On Dec. 14, 1775, the Convention ordered the Committee of Safety to employ captive slaves "in working the Lead Mine in the County of Fincastle, for the use of this Colony." Amer. Arch., 4th Ser., IV, 85. Shortly afterward four would-be followers of Dunmore who were captured at Accomac were ordered "sent up the country and employed in some publick works." Ibid., VI, 1553.

28. Ibid., VI, 1524.

had seized a schooner at Hungers Creek and sailed into the bay, their destination the James. Overtaken by a whale boat,[29] their execution was set for April 2, 1776. But the Northampton Committee of Safety sent word to Williamsburg inquiring whether the punishment should not be mitigated since the seizing of the boat was more "intended to effect an escape to Dunmore than any other Design of committing a felony."[30] Whenever the death sentence was passed, as in the case of two runaways who mistook an armed vessel of the Virginia navy for a British man-of-war, it was used mainly "as an example to others."[31]

Despite preventive efforts, whether an appeal to common sense or a resort to legal reprisals, many slaves made their way to the British, spurred in part by loyalist propaganda of the governor's good treatment.[32] Some two hundred "immediately joined him,"[33] and within a week after the proclamation the number had reached three hundred.[34] "Numbers of Negros and Cowardly Scoundrels flock to his Standard," wrote a member of the provincial Committee of Safety.[35] . . .

The Negroes who reached the British were generally able-bodied men who could be put to many uses.[36] It was as soldiers, however,

29. James Kent and William Henry to Maryland Council of Safety, Feb. 28, 1776, Arch. of Md., XI, 191.

30. Northampton Committee of Safety to General Committee of Safety, Apr. 23, 1776, "Va. Leg. Papers," Va. Mag. of Hist. and Biog., XV (Apr. 1908), 407.

31. Va. Gaz., Apr. 13, 1776.

32. Northampton Committee of Safety to General Committee of Safety, Apr. 23, 1776, "Va. Leg. Papers," Va. Mag. of Hist. and Biog., XV, 407. Dunmore would have every reason to welcome runaways, but perhaps his reception of them fell short of the report, circulated in the Virginia Gazette, that on the evening the governor's forces landed on Gwynn's Island, they amused themselves "with a promiscuous ball, which was opened, we hear, by a certain spruce little gentleman, with one of the black ladies." Va. Gaz., May 31, 1776.

33. Northampton Committee of Safety to Continental Congress, Nov. 25, 1775, "Va. Leg. Papers," Va. Mag. of Hist. and Biog., XIV (Jan. 1907), 251.

34. Andrew Sprowel to Peter Paterson, Nov. 19, 1775, ibid., XIV (Apr. 1907), 387.

35. John Page to Thomas Jefferson, Nov. 24, 1775, The Papers of Thomas Jefferson, ed. Julian P. Boyd (Princeton, 1950—in progress), I, 265.

36. Two women, however, were among a party of nine slaves who were seized in mid-December after putting out to sea in an open boat in an attempt to reach Norfolk. Pennsylvania Gazette, Philadelphia, Dec. 20, 1775.

that Dunmore envisoned them, and he enlisted them from the beginning. By early December he was arming them "as fast as they came in."[37] He made use of Negro privates at the rout of the colonials at Kemp's Landing; indeed, slaves had captured one of the two commanding colonels.[38] In the skirmishes preceding the action at Great Bridge, two runaways who were taken prisoner testified that the garrison was manned by thirty whites and ninety Negroes, and that "all the blacks who are sent to the fort at the great Bridge, are supplied with muskets, Cartridges &c strictly ordered to use them defensively & offensively."[39] By the first of December the British had nearly three hundred slaves outfitted in military garb, with the inscription, "Liberty to Slaves," emblazoned across the breast of each.[40] The governor officially designated them "Lord Dunmore's Ethiopian Regiment."[41]

. The first and only major military action in which Dunmore's forces were engaged was the battle of Great Bridge.[42] Of the governor's

37. Dunmore to Sec. of State for the Colonies, Dec. 6, 1775, Peter Force-George Bancroft Transcripts, "Virginia: Official Correspondence," Library of Congress.
38. Edmund Pendleton to R. H. Lee, Nov. 27, 1775, Amer. Arch., 4th Ser., IV, 202.
39. William Woodford to Edmund Pendleton, Dec. 5, 1775, "The Woodford, Howe, and Lee Letters," Richmond College Historical Papers, I (June 1915), 113. Added Woodford, "The bearer brings you one of the Balls taken out of the cartirages found upon the negro Prisoners, as they were extremely well made." Ibid., p. 112.
40. Maryland Gazette, Annapolis, Dec. 14, 1775.
41. Dunmore to Sec. of State for Colonies, Dec. 6, 1775, Force-Bancroft Transcripts.
42. Eyewitness accounts of the action at Great Bridge include: ". . . a Midshipman on board his Majesty's ship Otter, commanded by Captain Squires, Dec. 9," in Willard, Letters on the American Revolution, pp. 234–235; "Thomas McKnight to Rev. Dr. McKnight, on board the King's Fisher, Dec. 26, 1775," Miscellaneous Collection, Clements Library; "Contemporary English Accounts of the Destruction of Norfolk in 1776," comp. H. S. Parsons, Wm. & Mary Quart., 2d Ser., XIII (Oct. 1933), 219–224; Richard Kidder Meade to Theodorick Bland, Jr., Norfolk Town Camp, Dec. 18, 1775, in The Bland Papers, ed. Charles Campbell (Petersburg, 1840–43), I, 38; "The Woodford, Howe, and Lee Letters," Richmond College Hist. Papers, I, 96–163, passim; William Woodford to Edmund Pendleton, Dec. 10, 1775, in Md. Gaz., Dec. 21, 1775, and Jan. 4, 1776. For Dunmore's account see Dunmore to Secretary of State for the Colonies, Dec. 13, 1775, Force-Bancroft Transcripts. For the story, relished by Virginians, that a well-coached slave had been sent into Dunmore's lines with instructions to misrepresent the strength of the colonial militia, see John Burk, The History of Virginia (Petersburg, 1805–16), IV, 85.

troops of some six hundred men, nearly half were Negroes. Of the eighteen wounded prisoners taken by the Virginians in this rout, two were former slaves. James Anderson was wounded "in the Forearm— Bones shattered and flesh much torn," and Caesar was hit "in the Thigh, by a Ball, and 5 shot—one lodged."[43] After the fiasco at Great Bridge, the governor was forced to operate from his ships. Taking aboard the hardiest of his Negro followers and placing them under officers who exercised them at small arms, he sanguinely awaited recruits.

Dunmore's use of Negroes also embraced sailoring services. On the six tenders sent by the governor to cannonade Hampton in late October 1775, there were colored crewmen. Two of them were captured when the Virginians seized the pilot boat *Hawk Tender*.[44] To man the small craft that scurried in and out of the river settlements, harassing the plantations, the British depended largely on ex-slaves. Particularly were they needed as pilots. Joseph Harris, a runaway, served as pilot of the *Otter*, having come to Captain Matthew Squire with the highest recommendation from a fellow naval officer. "I think him too useful to His Majesty's service to take away," wrote the latter, because of "his being well acquainted with many creeks in the *Eastern* Shore, at *York*, *James* River, and *Nansemond*, and many others,..." and "accustomed to pilot...."[45] Two citizens on the Isle of Wight advised the chairman of the Virginia Committee of Safety to go slow on discharging "a Negro fello, named Caesar," who was not only "a very great Scoundrel" but was also "a fello' they can't do well without being an Excellent pilot."[46]

Another service performed by Dunmore's black followers was foraging. The governor's supply of provisions, particularly fresh foods, needed constant replenishing, and the Virginia leaders understandably would not permit the British to send men ashore to make pur-

---

43. Woodford to Pendleton, Dec. 10, 1775, "The Woodford, Howe, and Lee Letters," *Richmond College Hist. Papers*, I, 118.

44. John Page to Thomas Jefferson, Nov. 11, 1775, *Papers of Thomas Jefferson*, ed. Boyd, I, 257.

45. George Montague to Matthew Squire, July 20, 1775, *Amer. Arch.*, 4th Ser., II, 1692.

46. Thomas Pierce and Thomas Smith to Edmund Pendleton, Dec. 17, 1775, "Miscellaneous Colonial Documents," *Va. Mag. of Hist. and Biog.*, XIX (July 1911), 267.

chases. "Back settlers" who might have been willing to supply his lordship with provisions had "no means of conveying them,"[47] and Dunmore was driven to a dependence upon the foraging abilities of his Negro recruits. Marauding parties of predominantly ex-slave composition preyed on the countryside, making a night descent upon a plantation and making off with the choice livestock. One foraging party, captured while on its way to the Eastern Shore, was made up of "one white and sixteen blacks."[48]

Allegedly one of the services of Negroes to Dunmore was germ spreading. That the charge of germ warfare was propaganda-laden did not make it less potent in arousing indignation. The accusation was that Dunmore had inoculated two Negroes and sent them ashore at Norfolk to spread the smallpox.[49] The charge was ironic in view of the fate of the Negroes who fled to the British. The majority of them were disease fatalities. Late in March the governor informed his superior in England that the recruiting of the black regiment "would have been in great forwardness had not a fever crept in amongst them, which carried off a great many very fine fellows." He added that on advice of "medical people here," he had concluded that the trouble came from the overcrowded condition on the ships and the lack of clothing, both of which "we have now provided against."[50]

But the plague persisted, killing off the Negroes and the hope of the governor alike. Writing to Germain in June, Dunmore confessed defeat. The fever, he explained, was malignant, and had "carried off an incredible number of our people, especially blacks." Had this not happened he would have enlisted two thousand Negro followers. He was, ran his letter, separating the sick from the well and would try to keep the two groups from intermingling.[51] The governor's

---

47. "Extract of a letter to a gentleman in Scotland, dated Norfolk, Virginia, February 17, 1776," Amer. Arch., 4th Ser., IV, 1166.

48. Archibald Cary to R. H. Lee, Dec. 24, 1775, in Robert K. Brock, Archibald Cary of Ampthill (Richmond, 1937), p. 161.

49. Va. Gaz., June 15, 1776.

50. Dunmore to George Germain, Mar. 30, 1776, Amer. Arch., 5th Ser. (Washington, 1848–53), II, 159–160.

51. Dunmore to Germain, Mar. 30, 1776, Amer. Arch., 5th Ser., II, 162. Dunmore's policy of isolation appears to have prevented the smallpox from decimating the white troops. The monthly return of the 14th Regiment of

efforts were unavailing; by early June 1776 there were not more than "150 effective Negro men," although each day the black corps was augmented by from six to eight arrivals.[52]

The failure to arrest the smallpox, and the harassment by the Virginia and Maryland militia, finally brought an end to his lordship's stay in Chesapeake waters. In May 1776, faced with the likelihood "of a great reduction of our force" due to disease,[53] the fleet moved from their exposed quarters at Tucker's Mills near Portsmouth and took shelter on Gwynn's Island near the mouth of the Rappahannock. Nowhere were Dunmore and his "floating Town"[54] allowed peace; "we no sooner appear off the land, than signals are made from it," wrote Dunmore to Whitehall, "and if we come to anchor within cannonshot of either shore, guns are immediately brought to bear upon us. . . ."[55]

Early in July the British, after suffering an attack on their shipping, took refuge on St. George's Island in the Potomac. By the end of the month the disease-ridden corps, lacking suitable drinking water, and despairing of re-enforcements, prepared to make their exit. Dismantling, burning, or running aground sixty-three out of their 103 vessels, they sailed out of the Potomac on August 6, seven of the ships bound for Sandy Hook and the others setting a southward course for St. Augustine and the Bermudas.[56] With the departing

---

Infantry, signed by Capt. Sam Leslie, lists a total of 128 men (with breakdowns as to rank) for Mar. 1, 1776, a total of 126 men for Apr. 1, 1776, and a total of 122 for May 1, 1776. "Monthly Return of a Detachment of His Majesty's 14th Regiment of Infantry, off Norfolk, Virginia, 1 March 1776," Clinton Papers; *ibid.*, for Apr. 1, 1776, and for May 1, 1776. In addition to the factor of isolation, the mortality of the Negro soldiers may have been due to their performing most of the garrison and fatigue duties; at Gwynn's Island the entrenchments were guarded "chiefly by the black regiment," Va. Gaz., June 1, 1776.

52. Entry of June 10, 1776, A. S. Hamond Diaries, 1775–77, U. Va. library. Andrew Snape Hamond, captain of the *Roebuck*, was the commanding officer in Virginia waters.

53. *Ibid.*, May 19, 1776.

54. The descriptive phrase is Hamond's. Letter to Hans Stanley, Aug. 5, 1776, *ibid.*

55. Dunmore to George Germain, July 31, 1776, Amer. Arch., 5th Ser., II, 166.

56. Hamond Diaries, Aug. 6, 1776. Dunmore himself went to New York, arriving on Aug. 14. *Journals of Lieut.-Col. Stephen Kemble,* New-York Historical Society, *Collections* (1883–84), I, 84.

fleet went some three hundred Negroes, the healthiest going north-ward, destined for further military service, and Dunmore's schemes came to an inglorious end.[57]

Perhaps not more than a total of eight hundred slaves had suc-ceeded in reaching the British,[58] and perhaps one eighth of these had been brought by loyalist masters. But Dunmore's proclamation un-doubtedly had an indirect effect on thousands of additional slaves, quickening their hopes for freedom. Perhaps the imagination of colo-nial editors was behind such stories as that of a colored mother in New York naming her child after his lordship,[59] and that of a Negro in Philadelphia jostling whites on the streets and telling them to wait until "lord Dunmore and his black regiment come, and then we will see who is to take the wall."[60] But whether fact or fabrication, such reports reflect the attitude of expectation that Dunmore en-gendered among persons of color along the Chesapeake. It made no difference that he had offered freedom to the bondmen of his enemies only,[61] and that as governor he had withheld his signature from a bill against the slave trade; to those who whispered his name in slave quarters he was in truth the "African Hero" he was derisively dubbed by a Virginia patriot.[62]

If Dunmore was viewed by one group as a tyrant and by another as a liberator, this was but another paradox in a war that abounded in paradox, and another illustration of the war as a social revolution.

57. Dunmore remained convinced of the soundness of his plan to arm Negroes in large numbers, reviving it even after Yorktown. See Percy Burdelle Caley, "Dunmore: Colonial Governor of New York and Virginia, 1770–1782," unpubl. diss., University of Pittsburgh, 1939, pp. 887–893.

58. Dunmore's Negro followers were computed in general terms; e.g., ". . . came in a great number of Black men from the Rebels." Logs of *Roebuck* and *Fowey*, in Greenwich Museum, England, entry of June 27, 1776. Photostat in A. S. Hamond MSS., U. Va. library.

59. Taking due note, the *New York Journal* carried an occasional poem, copied in the Va. Gaz., May 25, 1776:
> Hail! doughty Ethiopian Chief!
> Though ignominious Negro Thief!
> This BLACK shall prop thy sinking name,
> and damn thee to perpetual fame.

60. Va. Gaz., Supplement, Dec. 29, 1775.

61. John King, runaway slave of a loyalist, was ordered discharged from the *King's Fisher*. Logs of *Roebuck* and *Fowey*, Feb. 23, 1776.

62. R. H. Lee to Thomas Jefferson, July 21, 1776, in *The Letters of Richard Henry Lee*, ed. James C. Ballagh (New York, 1912–14), I, 210.

The Negro who fled to the governor was actuated by the same love of freedom for which the colonists avowedly broke with the mother country. Dunmore's invitation to the slaves was to prefigure the thousands of runaways below the Mason-Dixon line who served as military laborers to His Majesty's forces during the Revolution and who, when peace came, sailed with them from Savannah, Charleston, and New York.

Reginald Horsman,
"American Indian Policy in the Old Northwest, 1783–1812"

The territorial settlement provided by the Treaty of Paris (1783)
which ended the American Revolution awarded the United States
not only the former thirteen colonies but also British holdings
between the Allegheny Mountains and the Mississippi River.
British policy which attempted to prevent American settlement
beyond the Alleghenies, mainly to keep peace between whites
and Indians, had long constituted a major colonial grievance. The
government and citizens of the new nation were well pleased
with the territorial settlement and eager to exploit the new lands.
But the Indians, who occupied the new territory and did not
recognize the claim of the United States government to it, presented
a barrier to the westward flow of white population. In "American
Indian Policy in the Old Northwest, 1783–1812," Reginald
Horsman analyzes the ways in which the United States attempted
to wrest the lands between the Ohio and Mississippi Rivers from
Indian control. Although the American government rapidly developed
a policy designed to minimize warfare between whites and
Indians, it is clear that it never deviated from its intention to
acquire most of the lands for white settlers.

American Indian Policy in the Old Northwest, 1783–1812

Reginald Horsman

In the years from 1783 to 1812 the one consistent element in American Indian policy in the Old Northwest was the desire to acquire the land between the Ohio and the Mississippi. The host of subsidiary objectives were all subordinated to this end. In theory, its attainment was simply a matter of telling the Indian inhabitants of the region that England had ceded it to the United States in 1783 and that the Indians could live only on lands allotted to them by the American government. In practice, it soon became apparent that the Indians were not prepared to acknowledge the English right to give away Indian land, and the Americans were obliged to obtain their objective in other ways. Between 1783 and 1812 the American government developed a policy that would secure land in the simplest and least expensive manner. Not only did it thus secure land, it also succeeded in convincing itself that what it was doing was in the best interests of the Indians. What had started out in 1783 as naked desire for land had, by 1812, been transmuted into lofty moral purpose. By 1812 American leaders were not only trying to convince

Abridged from Reginald Horsman, "American Indian Policy in the Old Northwest, 1783–1812," *William and Mary Quarterly*, XVIII (1961), pp. 35–53. Reprinted by permission of the author. Some footnotes have been renumbered.

others, but apparently had also convinced themselves that they were working for the ultimate benefit of the Indian. The manner in which national interest and moral purpose became entangled is a key to the history of nineteenth century expansion.

The first phase of post-Revolutionary American Indian policy in the Old Northwest lasted from 1783 to 1787. In the Treaty of Paris which ended the Revolution the British ignored their Indian allies. The Indians were left to make their own peace with the Americans, and their position was complicated by the fact that the Americans desired more than the cessation of hostilities in the Northwest. American frontiersmen had long since pushed into western Pennsylvania and down the Ohio to Kentucky. They were now anxious to settle the rich lands northwest of the Ohio. Moreover, the government of the Confederation had a financial interest in the movement of settlers into that region. By the sale of lands the Confederation hoped to solve its acute financial problems. It had already been agreed that the states with claims north of the Ohio would cede them to the central government, and by 1786 these cessions were accomplished. On October 10, 1780, Congress had promised that lands ceded to the United States would be disposed of for the common good, "and be settled and formed into distinct republican states."[1] Thus, in establishing peace with the Indians of the Northwest, the Confederation wished to begin the process of acquiring the lands between the Ohio and the Mississippi.

The document on which the Confederation based its Northwestern Indian policy from 1783 to 1787 was the report presented to Congress by James Duane, chairman of the committee on Indian affairs, on October 15, 1783. This resolved that a convention should be held with the Indians to make peace and establish boundary lines. The Indians were to be told that the land on which they lived had been ceded by Great Britain in the Treaty of Paris, and that as they had fought on the side of the British during the Revolution, they could justly be expelled to the north of the Great Lakes along with their allies. However, it was argued that America was prepared to forgive what was past and to draw a boundary line between the Americans and the Indians. As the United States needed land, both for her

1. Worthington C. Ford and others, eds., *Journals of the Continental Congress, 1774–1789* (Washington, 1904–37), XVIII, 915.

expanding population and for extinguishing her national debt, the Indians would have to cede a portion of their territory. This was justified as reparations for Indian hostility during the war. A boundary line was suggested that would have given most of the modern state of Ohio to the United States.[2] Though these suggestions were to be modified in detail, they formed the basis of policy until 1787.

The reasoning behind this report can best be understood by a consideration of letters sent to the committee on Indian affairs during the previous summer. The suggestions that most obviously influenced the committee were those made by George Washington and by General Philip Schuyler. Washington had twice written to express his views. In June 1783 he had supported the plan for establishing settlements of ex-soldiers in the west, arguing that the appearance of such formidable settlements in the vicinity of the Indian towns "would be the most likely means to enable us to purchase upon equitable terms of the Aborigines their right of preoccupancy; and to induce them to relinquish our Territories; and to remove into the illimitable regions of the West."[3] A far more comprehensive plan was submitted by Schuyler on July 29. He argued that America would be ill-advised to continue the war with the Indians to expel them from the country—it would cost a great deal, and the Indians would return if the force that expelled them should retire. Moreover, if driven to reside in British territory, the Indians would add strength to Great Britain. Even if America could expel the Indians at moderate cost, Schulyer argued, it would not be worth while. America should merely take the land she needed for present purposes: "It will be little or no obstacle to our in future improving the very country they may retain, whenever we shall want it. For as our settlements approach their country, they must from the scarcity of game, which that approach will induce to, retire farther back, and dispose of their lands, unless they dwindle comparatively to nothing, as all savages have done, who gain their sustenance by the chace, when compelled

2. *Ibid.,* XXV, 680–694. The boundary suggested was from the mouth of the Great Miami northward to its confluence with the Mad River, thence by a direct line to Fort Miami on the Maumee, and along the Maumee to Lake Erie. The committee that made this report consisted of James Duane, Richard Peters, Daniel Carroll, Benjamin Hawkins, and Arthur Lee.

3. To the President of Congress, June 17, 1783, John C. Fitzpatrick, ed., *The Writings of George Washington* (Washington, 1931–44), XXVII, 16–18.

to live in the vicinity of civilized people, and thus leave us the country without the expence of a purchase, trifling as that will probably be."[4] ...

The committee on Indian affairs ... paid close attention to the advice of Washington and Schuyler in its report of October 15, 1783, though needless to say the report did not mention that the drawing of a boundary line was intended as the prelude to the gradual extermination or expulsion of the Indians. In carrying out this policy in the following years, the Confederation stressed the idea that the Northwest had been ceded by the British, but it paid little attention to Washington's suggestion that the Indians should be conciliated in order to facilitate future land acquisition. Between 1783 and 1786 land northwest of the Ohio was acquired by three treaties—Fort Stanwix in 1784, Fort McIntosh in 1785, and Fort Finney in 1786. They were all dictated treaties. Though the extent of the land treated for was not as large as that envisioned by Congress originally, these negotiations resulted in the cession to the United States of what is now eastern and southern Ohio. . . .

Despite its apparent success, the Indian policy from 1783 to 1786 was disastrous. The United States not only proceeded on the assumption that the Indians should cede some of their land as retribution for their part in the Revolution, but also assumed that the territorial sovereignty granted by England in 1783 completely eliminated any Indian right to the soil of the Northwest. The Indians who inhabited the region naturally would not accept this interpretation of the Treaty of Paris. They could not conceive that the lands upon which they lived and hunted were not their own, and, moreover, during the colonial period they had become accustomed to the idea that the whites would purchase the Indian right to the soil in formal treaty. The American post-Revolutionary policy quickly produced Indian opposition. By 1786 hostilities were breaking out on the Northwest frontier, and the Indians were ready to fight to prevent American settlement northwest of the Ohio. The Shawnee almost immediately disavowed Fort Finney, and the Mohawk Joseph Brant was, with

---

4. To the President of Congress, July 29, 1783, Papers of the Continental Congress, No. 153, Letters of Schuyler, III, 601–607, National Archives, Washington, D. C.

British assistance, striving to unite the Northwestern tribes.[5] America had treaties to show her ownership of lands northwest of the Ohio, but in her straitened financial position she could not occupy and defend them.

An indication that force might soon be tempered by diplomacy came in the famous Northwest Ordinance of July 13, 1787. In regard to the intended acquisition of land from the Ohio to the Mississippi, the ordinance was perfectly in accord with previous policy. It laid down the system by which the land between those two rivers would come into the Union, and provided for not less than three nor more than five states in that area. This plan of course included the land allotted to the Indians between 1783 and 1786, in addition to Indian lands farther to the west. It was Article Three that foreshadowed a change in American thinking. "The utmost good faith shall always be observed towards the Indians," it stated; "their lands and property shall never be taken from them without their consent; and in their property, rights and liberty, they never shall be invaded or disturbed, unless in just and lawful wars authorised by Congress; but laws founded in justice and humanity shall from time to time be made, for preventing wrongs being done to them, and for preserving peace and friendship with them."[6]

Though the language of the ordinance seems so incongruous in view of what had gone before, the United States was in fact changing her policy in the summer of 1787. The objective of land acquisition remained the same, but the methods were to be modified. The change had been forced upon the United States by the extent of Indian resistance. On July 10, 1787, Secretary of War Henry Knox reported to Congress that there was neither sufficient money nor an adequate army to carry on an Indian war, Peace was essential.[7] Within two weeks Knox again told Congress of the precarious position and argued that it was better to spend a small sum on the

5. The growth of Indian resistance, and the encouragement given by the British is discussed in Randolph C. Downes, *Council Fires on the Upper Ohio: A Narrative of Indian Affairs in the Upper Ohio Valley until 1795* (Pittsburgh, 1940), 279 ff.

6. Clarence E. Carter, ed., *The Territorial Papers of the United States* (Washington, 1934—), II, 47, 39–50.

7. *Ibid.*, 31–35.

purchase of land than to fight an expensive Indian war.[8] Knox's report was referred to a congressional committee on Indian affairs, headed by Nathan Dane....

In accord with the suggestions of Knox and the committee, the United States moved toward a more diplomatic policy. On October 5 Congress acted on the committee report and recommended a general treaty. Later in the month it appropriated twenty thousand dollars for holding Indian treaties wherever Congress thought it necessary.[9] This sum was added to in the following years, and the United States attempted to follow a policy of purchase rather than conquest. However, the object of acquiring all the land to the Mississippi had not been abandoned—far from it. The instructions sent at the end of October 1787 to the governor of the Northwest Territory, Arthur St. Clair, told him: "You will not neglect any opportunity that may offer of extinguishing the Indian rights to the westward as far as the river Mississippi."[10]

The general treaty with the Indians, which was suggested as desirable in the summer of 1787, took a long time to accomplish. Neither the federation nor the Indians were noted for speed in negotiation, and it was not until the close of 1788 that Governor St. Clair met with the Indians at Fort Harmar on the Ohio in an attempt to bring peace to the Northwest. The council lasted into January 1789, and eventually St. Clair accomplished two treaties—one with the Six Nations and the other with the Wyandots, Delawares, Ottawas, and Chippewas. It was found impossible to obtain the boundaries suggested in St. Clair's instructions, but at least the new American policy was partially put into effect. In essence, St. Clair told the Indians that though the United States claimed the land by conquest she was prepared to pay for it as well....

Thus in the spring of 1789, when the Federal government came to

8. W. C. Ford, ed., *Journals of the Continental Congress*, XXXIII, 388–391.

9. *Ibid.*, 611–612, 665-666 (Oct. 12).

10. Secretary of Congress to St. Clair, Oct. 26, 1787, Carter, ed., *Territorial Papers*, II, 78–79. It was suggested that a suitable line might be one by which the Indians ceded everything south of a line drawn from the southern boundary of Pennsylvania to the Mississippi. On July 2, 1788, it was recommended that a better line might be the 41st degree of north latitude—this would have given considerably more to the United States all the way to the Mississippi; *ibid.*, 117. St. Clair realized that Indian resistance would make it impossible to obtain either line; *ibid.*, 130–132.

power, American policy was already changing in regard to the manner of acquiring lands. This change was to be accentuated by the new government. An immediate problem, however, was that the heavy-handed policy since 1783 had produced a crisis in the Northwest. The Fort Harmar treaty pleased the Indians no more than the treaties of Stanwix and McIntosh had done. It did nothing to solve the basic Indian dissatisfaction at losing their lands. Encouraged by the British, the Northwestern tribes were ready to insist once again upon an Ohio River boundary. They demanded that American settlers advance no farther.[11]

Henry Knox, who continued as Secretary of War, now made a determined effort to develop the new tendencies in American Indian policy. From this time forward the element of national honor played an increasingly important part in determining the methods of land acquisition. In a report of June 15, 1789, Knox urged negotiation rather than war. Even if the necessary force were available, he argued, it was debatable from the point of view of justice whether it would be wise to use it. In addition, he maintained that America did not have sufficient money to expel the Indians. Justice and expediency made negotiation essential. Knox estimated that to attach the Indians north and south of the Ohio to the United States for the next fifty years might cost $15,000 annually, whereas to coerce them would not only cost more money, but would also stain the character of the nation "beyond all pecuniary calculation." After these praiseworthy sentiments a rather more realistic calculation, reminiscent of Philip Schuyler's suggestion of July 29, 1783, entered into Knox's report: "As the settlements of the whites shall approach near to the Indian boundaries established by treaties, the game will be diminished, and the lands being valuable to the Indians only as hunting grounds, they will be willing to sell further tracts for small considerations. By the expiration, therefore, of the above period [fifty years], it is most probable that the Indians will, by the invariable operation of the causes which have hitherto existed in their intercourse with the whites, be reduced to a very small number."[12]

Several weeks later, in a report mainly concerned with the southern

11. At the Fort Harmar council the first Indian proposal had been for a boundary along the Ohio; see Draper MSS., 23U115–123.
12. *American State Papers, Indian Affairs,* I (Washington, 1832), 13–14.

Indians, Knox moved a step further in suggesting an acceptable Indian policy. He pointed out that in time there would probably be no Indians east of the Mississippi and he asked whether, instead of extermination, there should not be civilization of the Indians. He suggested the possibility of the use of missionaries and argued that even if this did not fully civilize the Indians, it would at least attach them to the American interest. To accomplish this, he also urged fair purchase from the Indians, the recognition of the Indian right of soil, the treatment of the Indian tribes as foreign nations, and the regulation of white emigration.[13] Knox was moving toward the idea that the acquisition of Indian land could be accomplished more easily, and with fewer pangs of conscience, if accompanied by a spreading of American civilization among the Indians and the protection of the Indians from brazen insult.

In the following years America was to pass various laws designed to protect the Indians from overt acts of violence and from exploitation. Regulations concerning the mode of white settlement, the encroachment on Indian land, the selling of liquor, and fair trading practices toward the Indians were all put into effect. These often did not work, owing to the problem of controlling the frontiersmen, but the American government was sincere in its effort to make them work. Everything possible was to be done to keep the Indians at peace. If fixed boundaries were established and peace were maintained, the land of the Northwest would eventually be absorbed by the American government at a small cost. Moreover, it would be absorbed in a manner that, it was presumed, would cast least discredit on the government.[14]

The irony of the situation was that the United States, though moving rapidly in 1789 toward a policy of peace and absorption, found it necessary to wage a five-year Indian war for which she had not the slightest desire. The Indians by 1789 were actively resisting the American advance—they did not want to yield any land beyond the Ohio either by war or purchase, and America would have to wage a successful campaign before she could put her desired policy into effect. General Josiah Harmar's defeat in 1790 made another campaign essential,

13. *Ibid.*, 52–54 (July 7, 1789).

14. A brief account of the governmental measures to prevent exploitation and injury of the Indians can be found in George D. Harmon, *Sixty Years of Indian Affairs . . . 1789–1850* (Chapel Hill, 1941), 18–19, 94–123.

and in 1791 St. Clair was sent into the Indian country. Secretary of State Thomas Jefferson expressed the position clearly in April 1791 when he said before St. Clair's expedition that "I hope we shall drub the Indians well this summer & then change our plan from war to bribery."[15] Unfortunately for the United States it was St. Clair who was drubbed, and this necessitated another three years of crisis before Anthony Wayne defeated the Indians at Fallen Timbers in August 1794. While these hostilities were proceeding, the American government advanced its plans to avoid such conflicts in the future.

In his messages to Congress, Washington advocated fair dealing with the Indians, impartial justice, reasonable trading practices, and strict regulation of the manner in which Indian lands might be obtained.[16] He also moved further in desiring the Americanization of the Indian. By 1792 the idea of teaching the Indians how to farm, to keep domesticated animals, and to build comfortable homes was entering into the instructions of American envoys to the Northwest....

The military victory of Anthony Wayne in August 1794 allowed the government to put into effect its desired Indian policy. Already, in April 1794, instructions in regard to the peace had been sent to Wayne. He was to obtain the boundaries of the Treaty of Fort Harmar and could confirm to the Indians their right of soil in the remainder of the Northwest. However, and this was vital, the United States must have the right of preemption.[17] According to the prevalent theories the Indians would inevitably want to sell more lands, and all the United States needed was the exclusive right to purchase them. This had been a *sine qua non* of peace with the Northwest Indians since the start of the new national government in 1789.[18]

15. To James Monroe, Apr. 17, 1791, Paul L. Ford, ed., *The Works of Thomas Jefferson* (New York, 1904–05), VI, 242.

16. See James D. Richardson, ed., *A Compilation of the Messages and Papers of the Presidents, 1789–1897* (Washington, 1896–99), I, 59, 104–105, 125–127, 141, 167, 185.

17. Knox to Wayne, Apr. 4, 1794, Northwest Territory Collection, William Henry Smith Library, Indianapolis, Indiana.

18. Though the United States was so anxious for peace, the Senate did not ratify the treaty made by Rufus Putnam with the Wabash tribes in Sept. 1792 on the grounds that it did not contain a clause guaranteeing the American right of preemption. See *American State Papers, Indian Affairs*, I, 338; *Journal of the Executive Proceedings of the Senate of the United States of America* (Washington, 1828—), I, 128, 134–135, 144–146.

Given the right of pre-emption, America inevitably would advance to the Mississippi.

When, in the spring of 1795, Wayne was near to the conclusion of a treaty with the Northwestern Indians, the new Secretary of War, Timothy Pickering, sent additional instructions for his guidance. Pickering explicitly renounced the policy pursued by the Confederation government in the post-1783 period—that is, the policy of claiming the Northwest by conquest—and said that the land belonged to the Indians. He stressed that peace and the satisfaction of the Indians were the most important considerations in the treaty. As a result the United States would claim little more land than had been obtained in 1789 at Fort Harmar.[19] This seems most reasonable unless another statement made by Pickering to Wayne is taken into consideration. "When a peace shall once be established," he wrote, "and we also take possession of the posts now held by the British, we can obtain every thing we shall want with a tenth part of the trouble and difficulty which you would now have to encounter."[20] He was paying his respects to the now well-established idea that if a boundary and peace were established Indian lands would soon fall into the hands of the Americans. . . .

The resounding phrases of the famous Treaty of Greenville thus meant very little. Though only eastern and southern Ohio, together with a strip of what is now southeastern Indiana, were granted to the United States, and though the United States relinquished her claims to all lands beyond these boundaries, it was quite evident to the American government that this was not a permanent division. Article Five gave the right of pre-emption in the remaining land of the Northwest to the United States—it was put in because it was quite obvious that it was going to be used. Moreover, by the treaty, the United States was given sixteen reservations of land on the Indian side of the boundary line to use as posts and was also granted free communication between them.[21] Indians throughout the Northwest were to have

19. Pickering to Wayne, Apr. 8, 1795, Richard C. Knopf, ed., *Campaign into the Wilderness: The Wayne-Knox-Pickering-McHenry Correspondence* (Columbus, Ohio, 1955), IV, 19–32.

20. Apr. 15, 1795, *ibid.*, 34.

21. *Statutes at Large of the United States of America*, VII (Boston, 1853), VII, 49–54.

the contact with white civilization that would result in their withdrawal or diminution in numbers. The Indians thought the Greenville line was to last forever, the Americans knew better. The territorial organization of the Northwest proceeded in spite of the Greenville line; in 1796 Wayne County was organized, stretching westward to Lake Michigan, and in 1800 the organization of the Indiana Territory also ignored the division made at Greenville.[22] The peace that reigned after Greenville allowed American settlers to pour into the ceded areas.

The period of calm lasted little longer than the administration of John Adams, for American settlers soon looked beyond the land ceded at Greenville. From 1801 to 1809 President Thomas Jefferson sought the land between the Ohio and the Mississippi rivers with all the eagerness of the Confederation. With the ambivalence that is so characteristic of Jefferson, he was able to combine an apparent genuine interest in the welfare of the Indian with a voracious appetite for Indian land. In his public utterances Jefferson viewed the harsh realities of American-Indian relations through a roseate mist. His first annual message, December 1801, expressed happiness that the Indians were becoming "more and more sensible" of the advantages of farming and "the household arts" over hunting and fishing.[23] The wish was apparently father to the thought. In the following month he told a visiting delegation of Miamis, Potawatomis, and Weas that the United States would "with great pleasure see your people become disposed to cultivate the earth, to raise heards of the useful animals and to spin and weave, for their food and clothing, these resources are certain, they will never disappoint you, while those of hunting may fail, and expose your women and children to the miseries of hunger and cold."[24] This became the rallying call of Jefferson throughout his presidency. He was convinced that the United States should take every opportunity to persuade the Indians to abandon their old modes of life. His motives were not entirely altruistic.

In January 1803 Jefferson submitted a message to Congress recom-

22. Carter, ed., *Territorial Papers*, II, 567–568, III, 86–88.

23. Richardson, ed., *Messages and Papers of the Presidents*, I, 326.

24. Jan. 7, 1802, War Department, Secretary's Office, Letters Sent, Indian Affairs, A, 143, National Archives, Washington, D. C.

mending the continuance of the system of American trading factories among the Indians.[25] He went on to comment upon American-Indian relations and told Congress that the Indian tribes had been growing increasingly uneasy at the diminution of their land, and that the policy of refusing to contract any further sales had been growing among them. To counteract this policy, "and to provide an extension of territory which the rapid increase of our numbers will call for," Jefferson recommended two measures. The first suggestion was to encourage the Indian tribes to abandon hunting and to engage instead in stock raising, agriculture, and domestic manufacture. He argued that it would be possible to show the Indians that by following this new way of life they could live better with less land and less labor. Their extensive forests would thus become useless to them, and they would see the advantage of exchanging these lands for the means of improving their farms and increasing their domestic comforts. His second suggestion was to multiply trading-houses among the Indians, "and place within their reach those things which will contribute more to their domestic comfort than the possession of extensive but uncultivated wilds." These measures would, he argued, prepare the Indians to share ultimately in the benefits of American government and civilization. "I trust and believe," stated Jefferson, "we are acting for their greatest good."[26] . . .

The transformation of the Indian into an American farmer, and the resulting surplus of land that would be happily yielded to the United States, was a vision which beset Jefferson throughout his two terms as president. Time and time again he told visiting delegations of Indians that the United States wanted them to abandon the difficulties of the chase and engage in the pleasures of farming. As game became increasingly scarce, he warned them, their families would starve.[27] Jefferson did not merely want the Indians to live in the

25. The Indian factory system had been established in 1796 to protect the Indians from unscrupulous traders, attach them to the United States, and counteract British and Spanish influence; see Ora K. Peake, A History of the United States Indian Factory System, 1795–1822 (Denver, 1954), passim.

26. Jan. 18, 1803, Richardson, ed., Messages and Papers of the Presidents, I, 352–353.

27. See messages from Jefferson to the various Indian tribes, War Dept., Secretary's Office, Letters Sent, Indian Affairs, A, 315, 413–415; B, 147–148, 279–282, 369–373, 394–397, 400–402, 410–413.

American manner, eventually he wanted them to be absorbed into the American population. He spoke of the ultimate point of rest and happiness for the Indians as being when the two races would become one people and when the Indians would become American citizens.[28] The Indians would throw off their own traditions and would assume those of the United States. The original aim of appropriating Indian land was now becoming inextricably entwined with the moralistic aim of bringing civilization to the Indians.

Thus Jefferson conjured up a dreamland in which the Indians would agree that the white man's civilization was superior and would be eager to yield their surplus lands to the expanding Americans. The fact is, of course, that Governor Harrison of Indiana, acting on instructions from Jefferson, pressed the Indians into selling a goodly portion of the modern states of Indiana and Illinois between 1802 and 1809....

While Jefferson spoke in his messages to Congress as though all this met with the approbation of the Northwestern Indians,[29] the intensity of their resistance was becoming increasingly obvious in the years after 1802. Rather than rushing forward to sell their surplus lands to taste the delights of agriculture, spinning, and weaving, the Indians were in these years becoming infuriated at the flouting of promises made at Greenville. By 1805 Tecumseh and the Prophet were beginning to organize resistance in the Northwest, and by the time Jefferson left office in 1809 the area was on the verge of war. In spite of this, Harrison in September 1809 secured yet another tract of land in Indiana.[30] This American pressure for land in the first decade of the nineteenth century greatly simplified the British task of preparing for the war that was to come in 1812. Though the British had deserted the Northwestern Indians in 1783 and in 1794, Indian anger at the American land policy insured that the Indians would once again be in the British camp.

Meanwhile Jefferson continued his policy of peace, civilization, and land appropriation. For a time, after the purchase of Louisiana in

28. To Benjamin Hawkins, Feb. 18, 1803, P. L. Ford, ed., Works of Jefferson, IX, 445–449.

29. Richardson, ed., Messages and Papers of the Presidents, I, 343–344, 359, 371–372, 386–387.

30. Statutes at Large, VII, 113–116.

1803, he toyed with the possibility of removal west of the Mississippi as a solution to the Indian problem, but his interest in this project soon faded.[31] To the end of his second term, his desire for land, and the linked desire of civilizing the Indians, continued unassuaged. . . .

In December 1808 he told the Miami chief, Little Turtle, of the advantage of agriculture over hunting, and then continued by saying that "I have therefore always believed it an act of friendship to our red brethren whenever they wished to sell a portion of their lands, to be ready to buy whether we wanted them or not—because the price enables them to improve the lands they retain and turning their industry from hunting to agriculture the same exertions will support them more plentifully."[32] It would seem that Jefferson had come to believe that not only was the civilization of the Indian convenient for acquisition of land, but that he was also acquiring land in order to civilize the Indian.

Shortly before he left office he spoke with conviction, and with an eloquent peroration, when he told an assembled gathering of Northwestern Indians: "I repeat that we will never do an unjust act towards you. On the contrary we wish you to live in peace, to increase in numbers, to learn to labor as we do and furnish food for your ever encreasing numbers, when the game shall have left you. We wish to see you possessed of property and protecting it by regular laws. In time you will be as we are: you will become one people with us: your blood will mix with ours: and will spread with ours over this great island. Hold fast then my children, the chain of friendship which binds us together: and join us in keeping it forever bright and unbroken."[33]

American Indian policy in the Northwest during these hectic years revolved around the problem of the acquisition of land. The Confederation government first tried the simple methods of force, and discovered there was no surer way of producing Indian war. Anxious to avoid war, from financial as well as humanitarian motives, the Confederation turned to a policy of purchase, which involved the

31. See Annie H. Abel, "The History of Events Resulting in Indian Consolidation West of the Mississippi," American Historical Association, *Annual Report . . . 1906* (Washington, 1908), I, 241 ff.

32. War Dept., Secretary's Office, Letters Sent, Indian Affairs, B, 400–401.

33. To chiefs of the Wyandots, Ottawas, Chippewas, Potawatomis, and Shawnee, Jan. 1809, *ibid.*, B, 412–413.

recognition of Indian rights to land beyond certain boundary lines. Recognition of this right did not mean that America expected any difficulty in acquiring further areas of land. The government acted on the assumption that the pressure of white population up to the de-marcation line would produce a diminution in game, a reduction in the Indian population, and a desire to sell land cheaply. The new federal government inherited this policy from the Confederation and added to it. The most important addition was a more acute awareness that the national honor was involved. An attempt was made to give the Indians as much justice as was compatible with the wholesale acquisition of land. In fact, the government was prepared to defend the Indian against everyone except itself. In the 1790's there was a growing governmental interest in the possibility of bringing civiliza-tion to the Indian—that is, in transforming him into an American farmer. There seems to have been little realization that the Indian might not consider this an advantage. From the American point of view it was an ideal solution, for the Indian would cede his vast lands, and what was left of the Indian population would be absorbed into American civilization. This concept received far greater development after 1800 during the presidency of Thomas Jefferson. Though com-paratively little progress was made in this direction, Jefferson acted as if the whole program was taking tremendous strides and proceeded to support William Henry Harrison in the acquisition of considerable areas of land. He never seemed to realize the wide discrepancy be-tween the lofty nature of his aims and the rather sordid land-grabbing that was taking place in the Northwest.

The basic object of American Indian policy in this period—the acquisition of land—was a striking success. The subsidiary aims of peace, friendship, and the eventual absorption of the Indian into the American way of life resulted in failure. This failure was to be re-peated throughout American history, for wholesale land acquisition and friendship with the Indians were incompatible. However much members of the government might desire to win the friendship of the Indians, they could only do so by establishing a permanent barrier to the expansion of the American population over the North American continent. This would have meant leaving the area to the Indians, who were considered savages by the majority of the American people. While Indians roamed freely over the rich Mississippi Valley, the United States would have confined its rapidly increasing population to the eastern portion of its internationally recognized boundaries. Even if the government had desired such a policy, it could hardly have enforced it. Thus the American government was forced into the dilemma of trying to reconcile wholesale land acquisition and justice to the Indians. The dilemma was never solved—probably because it was insoluble—and America discovered very early in her history that the lot of a colonizer with a conscience is not a happy one.

Kenneth W. Porter,
*"Florida Slaves and Free Negroes
in the Seminole War, 1835–1842"*

During the early nineteenth century, the white citizens of Florida
lived surrounded by two hostile nonwhite groups—blacks, both
free and slave, and Seminole Indians. The white nightmare of
a red and black coalition against Caucasian domination became a
reality during the Seminole War. Kenneth Porter, in "Florida
Slaves and Free Negroes in the Seminole War, 1835–1842,"
describes the nonwhite resistance to the United States government
which blossomed into the most protracted Indian War in American
history. He demonstrates that the Seminole revolt against the
policy of Indian removal was significantly strengthened by the
cooperation of slaves seeking freedom and free blacks who feared
enslavement. Although the military power and duplicity of the
government ultimately prevailed, many blacks secured their freedom
by their spirited resistance.

Florida Slaves and Free Negroes in the Seminole War, 1835-1842

Kenneth W. Porter

At the outbreak of the Seminole War, the Negroes of Florida were divided into three categories: slaves to the whites, principally on the sugar plantations of the St. John's valley; free Negroes, the result of the lenity of the Spanish law which required the emancipation of any slave offering his master $300, principally in St. Augustine and vicinity; and "Indian Negroes," living among the Seminole, either as legal slaves, through purchases from Spaniards, English, or Americans, or, in a greater number of cases, runaways and their descendants, but all thoroughly identified in customs and interests with the Indians, at the worst as their favored dependents, at the best as advisers to the chief men of the tribe, and in no case treated as chattels.

The Seminole War, ostensibly caused by the insistence of the United States government on the removal of the Seminole to the Indian Territory, along with most of the other Indian tribes east of the Mississippi, in order to make room for white settlers and prevent border difficulties, was in large measure also urged on by the desire of slave traders and slave owners to gain possession of the

Abridged from Kenneth W. Porter, "Florida Slaves and Free Negroes in the Seminole War, 1835–1842," pp. 390–421. Copyright © by The Association for the Study of Negro Life and History, Inc. Published in *The Journal of Negro History*, XXVIII (January 1943). Some footnotes have been renumbered.

114

Negroes living among the Seminole; on the other hand, the unwillingness of the Indians to leave the country in which they had established themselves was reinforced by the fear of the Seminole Negroes lest, emerging from their fastnesses for transportation to the west, they should be seized and enslaved.

All the parties to the controversy were well acquainted with one another. There had been peace between the whites and the Seminole ever since the annexation of Florida to the United States. The Indians and their Negroes had been accustomed to come frequently into St. Augustine and other towns to trade, and were familiar with the city and its inhabitants. Racial ties made the relations among the various categories of Florida Negroes particularly close. Many of the slave-men "had wives among the Indian negroes, and the Indian negroes had wives among them."[1] . . .

As 1835 drew to a close it became evident that arrival at a state of open hostilities was only a matter of time. Military preparations for the forcible removal of the Indians were countered by sporadic raids and murders on the part of the Seminole. The white people of Florida did not, in general, however, regard the future very seriously. They considered the Seminole an essentially peaceful, even rather cowardly people, whose resistance could be abated in a few weeks; the war actually lasted for nearly seven years and proved to be the most protracted and expensive "Indian war," both in lives and money, which the United States has ever undergone. The Floridians, and the people of the United States in general, had overlooked or underestimated the Negroes—Indian Negroes, plantation slaves, free Negroes—as a factor of resistance. They were to be speedily disillusioned and enlightened. . . .

When, late in December, 1835, hostilities broke out on a large scale, it was evident that they had been carefully prepared and coordinated by the savage enemy. The St. John's River Indians, under their chief Emathla, or King Philip as the whites called him, ably seconded by his Negro associate and subordinate John Caesar, fell upon the plantations of that region on the night of Dec. 26-27, plundering and burning,[2] while on the morning of Dec. 28, Maj.

1. *Douglas, Thomas, Autobiography of,* N. Y. 1856, pp. 120–123.
2. *Niles Register,* vol. xlix, p. 369; "A Lieutenant of the Left Wing," *Sketch of the Seminole War,* Charleston, 1836, pp. 19–20.

Dade's company of over one hundred men was annihilated on the march from Ft. Brooke (Tampa) to Ft. King (Ocala) by the Seminole of the Tampa and Withlacoochee region, led by head chief Micanopy, his war leader and nephew Alligator, his chief counsellor and brother-in-law Jumper, and his Negro adviser Abraham; Louis Pacheco ne Fatio, the slave who had been hired as a guide for the expedition, is generally said to have been in communication with the hostiles and to have assisted in the destruction of the troops, although in his old age, fifty-seven years later, he stoutly denied the charge.

The horror caused by the almost complete destruction of an entire command, including many well-known and popular officers, paled beside that inspired by the enthusiasm with which the plantation slaves rallied to the insurgent Seminole. From plantation after plantation came the menacing word. "Depeyster's negroes were traitors, and must have been in league with the Indians; they assisted them with a boat to cross over to Dummett's ... the whole of Major Heriot's and Depeyster's negroes ... moved off with the Indians." "Upwards of two hundred and fifty negroes ... have joined the Indians and are more desperate than the Indians." Some of the Depeyster Negroes had painted their faces in symbol of their new allegiance. It was cold comfort even to learn that "Anderson's negroes behaved with the utmost prudence and fidelity," concealing as much as possible of their master's property before fleeing, for the reporter went on to announce gloomily that even this loyalty would be of little ultimate value, since the Negroes of neighboring plantations would, of course, readily discover this *cache* and reveal it to the foe. That the plantation Negroes were joining the Indians, Gen. Hernandez understandably declared, "is the very worst feature of the whole of this war."[3] ...

The situation appeared serious enough to the St. Augustinians, into whose city were crowding the frightened or sullen refugees, white and black, from the devastated plantations to the south. But westwardly, where more than one serious action had already been

3. *The Charleston Courier,* Jan. 12, 21, 22, 1836; National Archives, War Department, Adjutant General's Office, Maj. Benjamin A. Putnam, Cantonment Rosetta, Dec. 29, 1835, to Brig. Gen. J. M. Hernandez, St. Augustine (316), Putnam, Bulowville, Jan. 4, 1836, to Hernandez (25), Hernandez, Dec. 30, 1835, to Lewis Cass (H129/316).

fought by the beginning of 1836, and where the United States posts were closely invested, it was really critical. The commander at Ft. Brooke, from which the Dade command had marched so confidently, announced, a week after its wiping out: "This place is invested by all the Florida Indians in the field, with a large accession of Negroes, particularly from the plantations of Tomoka & Smyrna, as appears from the examination of a prisoner just taken."[4] . . .

In St. Augustine, where the planters, together with such of their Negroes as had not the desire or ability to "move off" with the Seminole, had taken refuge, they, and their fellows in the immediate vicinity, were still exposed to the dangers presented by the Negro-Indian alliance, actual or potential. With several hundred Negroes concentrated within the walls of the city, most of whom "had . . . for years lived on the frontier in the neighborhood of the Indians" and "spoke their language," "strong apprehensions were felt . . . that they would fire the town, and that, during the confusion resulting . . . ; the Indians might rush in." Patrols were organized to cope with this menace, but arms of any sort were almost non-existent and it was discovered that during the few weeks preceding the outbreak the Indians had purchased nearly all the powder and lead available in the local shops.[5]

In addition to an actual attack by the Seminole, in cooperation with Negro sympathizers in the town, the whites of St. Augustine had to guard against communications between the hostile Indians and Negroes without and potential allies among the Negroes within. Emissaries of the enemy endeavored to enter the town to induce Negroes to join them and to obtain information, and Negroes within the town endeavored to escape through the lines to join the Seminole, carrying with them knowledge of the plans of the whites, and sometimes supplies. In recognition of this Negro-Indian alliance the Territory of Florida passed an act, "respecting hostile negroes & mulattoes in the Seminole nation," providing that any free persons belonging to those categories who should be captured should be sold into slavery as a punishment. . . .

It cannot, of course, be claimed that all the plantation slaves, even

4. National Archives, War Department, AGO, Capt. F. S. Belton, Ft. Brooke, Jan. 5, 1836, to the Adjt. Gen. (23).
5. Douglas, loc. cit.

those who had the opportunity, aligned themselves with the Seminole. A considerable number of the Indians themselves were, from the first, supporters of the United States government rather than of the cause of their own people. The same cannot be said of the Seminole Negroes, who, apparently to a man, maintained the cause of liberty until the background of resistance was broken and the principal chiefs had begun to surrender. The Negroes who were living among the whites had no such freedom of decision, and reacted according to circumstances and individual differences....

In the meantime, while the citizens of St. Augustine were endeavoring to deal with the "enemy within their gates," the first year of the Seminole War was drawing to a close, a year during which neither party had won a decisive advantage but in which, nevertheless, the Negro-Indian allies had at least held their own and perhaps maintained a slight superiority. It was a year, too, in which the Negroes, particularly, of course, the Indian Negroes but not neglecting the recent runaways, had borne their full share of the burden and heat of the day. "Micanopy, Philip, and Cooper ... are about a day's march from each other, each with from one hundred and twenty to two hundred Indian and negro warriors—the latter perhaps the more numerous," wrote on Dec. 9, 1836, Gen. Thomas Sidney Jesup, the newly appointed commander. "This, you may be assured," he continued, "is a negro, not an Indian war; and if it be not speedily put down, the south will feel the effects of it on their slave population before the end of the next season."[6] ...

But early in 1837, under Gen. Jesup's vigorous leadership, the United States troops and state militia struck a series of staggering blows at the Indian-Negro enemy, Osceola's force, in particular, being completely disrupted. It was at this time that John Caesar, the Indian Negro partisan leader, operating in the St. John's region, began a diversion which might well have been important—a series of guerrilla raids on plantations which extended almost up to the very gates of St. Augustine....

... That a band composed almost entirely of Negroes should have the temerity to attempt a raid in the immediate vicinity of St. Augustine ... and that the hostile Negroes should be ... conclusively

6. *American State Papers, Military Affairs,* vol. vii, pp. 820–821; 25th cong., 2nd sess., 1837–38, h. ex. doc., vol. iii, no. 78, p. 52.

demonstrated to be in . . . close and constant communication with the Negro population of the city, revived something of the panic of the early days of the war.

The city council, Jan. 23, 1837, accordingly passed "An ordinance to prevent the selling of ammunition to Slaves, free Negroes & molattos," which it is rather surprising to learn had not already long since been forbidden.[7] Stephen Merritt *alias* Wright, . . . and Randall Irving, free persons of color, were indicted at the Superior Court "for treason against the United States, in supplying the Seminole Indians with provisions and ammunition. They were arraigned and pleaded not guilty."[8] The fears of the citizenry were not perceptibly diminished by the capture, in March, of one of the principal malefactors.

Andrew Gue [Gay] . . . belonging to Col. Gue of this city, who ran away from his master in June last, was captured on Thursday morning at 4 A.M. by a detachment of six men under Lieut. John Ferreira, of Capt. Hudson's company of Mounted Volunteers. Andrew is a young negro not exceeding 21 years of age, and active and enterprising. He went off, joined the Indians, and after being with them for some weeks, he returned clandestinely to town, and held a meeting with some of his friends and enticed some of them off. At this meeting he stated that he had become high in the confidence of the Indians and he only wanted a white man's scalp to make him a great man. On several occasions since he has made his appearance in the vicinity, and was with the gang of negroes when Capt. Hopson [Hanson?] killed John Caesar,[9] at which time he received three wounds. He says he bled considerable, and since

7. "Minutes of the City of St. Augustine, Nov. 18, 1836–Nov. 15, 1854," City Building, St. Augustine, Fla., p. 8.

8. *The Daily National Intelligencer* (Washington, D. C.), Apr. 17, 1837. There is no record of either of these cases in the above-mentioned *Inventory*.

9. This must refer to the episode of January, and John Caesar must have been one of the two Indian Negroes killed; Andrew doubtless identified him after his own capture. No other encounter corresponding to this description is known to have taken place. For a description of John Caesar's career prior to the final episode in his life, see the author's "John Caesar: A Forgotten Hero of the Seminole War," *The Journal of Negro History*, vol. xxviii (Jan., 1943), pp. 53–65. At the time of writing this article, the author was unaware of the circumstances of John Caesar's death, though, of the three possibilities advanced, one comes pretty close to the facts as now known.

that time he has not seen or spoken to any person whatever. He has remained in the neighborhood of the place where he was wounded, subsisting on roots, &c., until he was induced from hunger to come to our neighborhood for provisions, and which led to his capture.[10]

Andrew was duly committed to prison, but even the knowledge that this dangerous character was behind bars and that the formidable John Caesar would no longer trouble the country, seems to have been of little comfort, compared with the uneasiness produced by the knowledge that there were at large other runaway slaves,[11] who, like Andrew Gay, might be longing for a white man's scalp, and with the ability to penetrate into the midst of the town to plot insurrection with their fellows, and imbue them with a desire for similar trophies. The city council on May 2 passed a resolution that Capt. Hanson's company, which had done such good service in hunting down and breaking up John Caesar's band, should be recalled and "employed to scour the country in the neighborhood"—"from within our own community," a resolution of a month later declared, "we know not how soon firebrands may be thrown amongst us," and the necessity for all to join in the defense of the city was stressed.[12] Thus the fear of a slave insurrection operated to keep the militia companies near home, deprived Gen. Jesup of their assistance, and relieved the pressure on the Negroes and Indians actually in the field. To that extent John Caesar, [the free Negro] Joe Merritt, Andrew Gue or Gay, and their fellows had not shed their blood in vain.

From the last of January to the first of June, 1837, it had seemed probable that hostilities might be speedily and permanently terminated. The war had been going badly for the Seminole and to Gen. Jesup the time seemed ripe for peace negotiations. But he recognized that the terms could not be too onerous, since "in all the numerous battles and skirmishes that have taken place, not a single first-rate

10. *The Charleston Courier*, Mar. 21, 1837. I have been unable to find any record of this case elsewhere, or any information as to Andrew's fate; his case is not listed in the *Inventory*.

11. *Ibid*. One such runaway was named Smart, and belonged to the late Pablo Salvate, having gone off the previous summer. He was detected lurking in the vicinity and may have been a member of the disrupted John Caesar band.

12. St. Augustine minutes, pp. 11, 13.

warrior has been captured, and only two Indian men have surrendered. The warriors have fought as long as they had life, and such seems to be the determination of those who influence their councils —I mean the leading negroes." Accordingly he communicated through a captured Indian Negro, Ben, with the principal Negro leader, Abraham, and through him got in touch with other principal chiefs, Indian and Negro. On March 6, 1837, an agreement was signed providing that "the Seminoles and their allies, who come in and emigrate West, shall be secure in their lives and property; [and] that their negroes, their bona fide property, shall also accompany them West."[13] This was understood by the Seminole as protecting not only the Negroes to whom some of the Indians might have a more or less valid title, but also "their allies," the other Negroes who were then living among them and fighting with them, and at first Gen. Jesup had insisted on that interpretation. "The negroes," that is, the Indian Negroes, "rule the Indians," he wrote on March 26, 1837, "and it is important that they should feel themselves secure; if they should become alarmed and hold out, the war will be renewed."[14] Obviously, any attempt to meddle with any of the Negroes who had been fighting in the Seminole ranks for over a year would arouse apprehension among the others. But Gen. Jesup's decision that the runaway Negroes among the Seminole were "their allies" and protected by the terms of the capitulation, was inevitably greeted with violent protest by planters who had lost slaves during the war, and finally, yielding to their pressure, he was induced to make a clandestine arrangement on April 8 with certain Indian chiefs, notably Coi Hajo, second chief of the St. John's River Seminole, "to surrender the negroes taken during the war,"[15] thus endeavoring to

---

13. ASP, MA, vii, 825–828; *Army and Navy Chronicle*, iv, 80.

14. ASP, MA, vii, 835.

15. *Niles Register*, Apr. 29, 1837, p. 133. See: Giddings, Joshua, *The Exiles of Florida*, Columbus, O., 1858, ch. xi, for a detailed discussion of this agreement. Although Coi Hajo had participated in the Seminole resistance to removal, he had been looked on, prior to the outbreak of the war, as weak-kneed in his opposition—so much so that it is said that it had been intended to put him to death along with Chalo (Charley) Emathla, leader of the emigration party. National Archives, AGO, Bvt. Lieut. Col. A. C. W. Fanning, Ft. King, Nov. 28, 1835, to Brig. Gen. D. L. Clinch, St. Augustine (478). It is possible that jealousy of Philip, head chief of the St. John's River Seminole, may partially account for some of the divagations of the second chief.

introduce a division, based on the time of their escape, into the ranks of the Negroes among the Seminole....

What was in the wind could not be long kept from the nostrils of those principally concerned. Not all the Negroes with the Indians had, of course, joined them entirely of their own free will, and many of those who had been eager enough at first had by this time no doubt become tired of the bargain. The Indians themselves had suffered severely from lack of food and clothing, and the less-experienced plantation Negroes had not, of course, been any better off, probably a good deal worse. Those who had not displayed any particular enthusiasm for defending their newly acquired liberty with arms in their hands had been sent off, with the women, old men, and children, to secluded islands and hammocks, and put to raising corn; they may well have felt that they had merely exchanged one slavery for another, almost as arduous and even less rewarding in physical comforts. Those who felt thus did not need to be "brought in"; they eagerly surrendered themselves whenever the approach of a body of troops gave them the opportunity, hoping that the excuse of having been "captured" would save them from punishment. A dozen Negroes who surrendered in May were clad only in ragged muddy breech cloths and complained that they had been forced to live entirely on koonti-roots, from which the Indians made a sort of bread, and on alligator tails, and that when things were going badly for the Indians they had sometimes vented their ill-temper on the Negroes by beating them.[16]

Other Negroes prized their freedom higher than considerations of immediate comfort. Lt. Col. W. S. Harney wrote on May 16 that "there was a party [of Negroes] on Cedar Creek who were all runaways and [when they learned that they were to be returned to their masters] resisted telling the Indians that they [the Indians] had not taken them & that they [the Negroes] would not give up."[17] Negroes of this mind and spirit received support from the more militant Indians, such as Osceola. Some of the Negroes who surrendered reported that Coi Hajo had announced in council that the runaway Negroes were to be returned, whereupon Osceola, rising in a rage,

16. Motte, Capt. J. Rhett, "Life in Camp and Field," St. Augustine Historical Society (ms.), p. 161.
17. Florida Historical Society (photostat).

declared that so long as he was in the nation it should never be done.[18] ...

The determined opposition of Osceola and other militant chiefs, and the resistance of freedom-loving Negroes who had gotten wind of Coi Hajo's plot with Gen. Jesup, naturally checked or diminished the movement toward Tampa Bay, particularly of Negroes, whether "Indian" Negroes or "captured." Even the Indian Negroes already assembled at Tampa Bay became uneasy as persons owning, or claiming to own, slaves who had taken refuge among the Indians, began to appear at the emigration camp. Many of the Indian Negroes were themselves runaways, though of long standing, or the children of runaways, and thus legally slaves, whatever the terms or interpretation of Gen. Jesup's already once-broken agreement. Finally, early in June, under the instigation and leadership of Osceola, Wild Cat, and the young Indian Negro chief John Cavallo, most of the Indian Negroes and many Indians fled the camp, taking with them, for good measure, the principal hostages they had given for the fulfillment of the Ft. Dade capitulation.[19]

Too late Gen. Jesup recognized his error. Most of the Indians and Negroes would probably have eventually surrendered to be sent out of the country had he not spoiled everything by trying to force the surrender of recent runaways. He had secured by this policy about a hundred each of Indian Negroes and runaways, but now the war was revived, with a greater danger than ever, in the general's opinion, of spreading to the plantations. "The two races," he wrote in June, "the negro and the Indians, are rapidly approximating; they are identified in interests and feelings"—and it is evident that Gen. Jesup is here speaking of the slave Negro, not the Indian Negro, whose "identity" with the Indian was too self evident to require comment....

Only a sense of humiliation, resulting from the failure of his carefully worked out plans of early 1837, and driving him nearly to desperation, can explain—it cannot justify—several of Gen. Jesup's actions in the autumn of that year and early in the following. The fortunate capture in September of Philip (Emathla), the St. John's

18. 1st Lieut. R. H. Peyton, May 24, 1837, to Harney, Florida Historical Society (photostat).
19. ASP, MA, vii, 371.

River head chief, made it possible to use him as a bait to attract, for conversation with his father, his favorite son Wild Cat, who was then employed as an emissary to draw in about a hundred Negroes and Indians, including several chiefs and sub-chiefs, among them those irreconcilables Osceola and John Cavallo, supposedly for a conference. Instead they were surrounded and captured. About twenty, including Wild Cat and John Cavallo, escaped the next month, but it was nonetheless a serious blow. Over a hundred others, including the head chief Micanopy, were seized by a similar device early in December and, discouraged by this, still others surrendered. But there were still enough hostiles in the field, under Wild Cat, Alligator, Sam Jones, and John Cavallo, to fight the most seriously contested action of the war, on Christmas Day, at Lake Okeechobee, against Col. Zachary Taylor. Gen. Jesup himself took the field next month and fought an action on the Laxahatchie west of Okeechobee—a battle in which an officer said there were as many Negroes as Indians among the Seminole warriors.[20]

Jesup now considered the time ripe to re-open peace negotiations. He had learned wisdom in the months since the previous June. He suggested to the Indians that they *might* be allowed to remain on a reservation in southern Florida, but said nothing about returning runaway slaves. He was becoming more and more convinced of the inadvisability of returning captured Negroes to servitude. He had hired a considerable number of Creek mercenaries, promising them as plunder all the Negroes they could capture, but when, in September, 1837, they succeeded in capturing eighty, he wrote: "It is highly important to the slaveholding States that these negroes be sent out of the country, and I would strongly recommend that they be sent to one of our colonies in Africa," i.e., Liberia. These Negroes were accordingly taken from the Creeks, and a "reward" of $20 per head substituted, much to the latter's dissatisfaction.[21] The Negroes were eventually sent not to Liberia but to the Indian Territory; in either case their freedom was assured.

Jesup also addressed himself directly to the Seminole Negroes, endeavoring to drive a wedge between them and the Indians, as he had previously striven to separate the Seminole, both Indian and

20. Motte, op. cit., p. 255.
21. ASP, MA, vii, 882.

Negro, from the recently escaped slaves. He issued an order "that all the property of the Seminole Indians in Florida at war with the United States who separated themselves from the Indians, and delivered themselves up to the Commanding officer of the troops, should be free"—an early and oddly-placed Emancipation Proclamation. Gen. Jesup's idea was now to send the Seminole Negroes to the Indian Territory with those who had already been transported, and put the Indians on a reservation in a remote part of the peninsula, trusting that its inaccessibility to the plantation region, and the absence of Negroes therein, would prevent its becoming a haven for runaways. He explained that "Separating the negros from the Indians weaken[s] the latter more than they would be weakened by the loss of the same number of their own people"[22]—evidence that Jesup still held to his original opinion that the Seminole Indian War might more appropriately be entitled the Negro War. Slavery among the Seminole was not so onerous that this offer in itself was probably of much effect; its importance lay in the suggestion that Jesup was now willing to make a special effort to conciliate the Negro element among the Seminole. In response to Jesup's invitation nearly 700 Seminole, about a fourth Negroes, assembled at Ft. Jupiter for a conference, but in the meantime the Secretary of War had refused to consider any peace except on the basis of emigration, so the general, probably against his real inclinations, accomplished another master-piece of treachery by arresting the entire lot. This discouraged the others so that 450 more, one-third of them Negroes, surrendered shortly after. On March 13 Jesup announced that "nearly all the blacks have left the field, by capture or surrender."[23] The only Negro chief who had not surrendered or been captured was John Cavallo, and he, with Alligator, the Indian chief with whom he was most closely associated, came in early in April, at the general's special invitation and promise of freedom.[24] Again it seemed that the war was over, and in May, Gen. Jesup was retired and was replaced by Zachary Taylor.

But, though nearly all the principal chiefs were dead or prisoners,

22. National Archives, Department of the Interior, Indian Bureau, Florida (Emigration) File A1282-1842, Statement of Brig. Gen. Zachary Taylor, Ft. Brooke, Apr. 30, 1840; ibid., Seminole File W244-1848, T. S. Jesup, near Ft. Jupiter, Feb. 28, 1838, to Brig. Gen. R. Jones, Washington.

23. A. & N. C., vi, 190.

24. N. R., May 5, 1838; A. & N. C., vi, 300, 315.

several minor chiefs, now, if only for want of competition, become of major importance, were left to carry on the fight—including one, who, for over a year, had been steadily increasing in stature until he could be recognized without qualification as of the first rank— Wild Cat or Coacoochee. After the Battle of Lake Okeechobee he had moved north to his old stamping-ground on the St. John's. Included in his band were a number of recent runaways from that region, and his expert utilization of their services as spies was known and commented upon by his adversaries.[25] He also, as before, found willing allies among the Negro population, slave or free, within the lines of the forces of slavery. . . .

During William J. Worth's command the war was finally, in August, 1842, brought to an official and, this time, permanent conclusion—if thirteen years, the time elapsing between the end of the Second Seminole War and the outbreak of the Third, suffice for permanency. This was accomplished partly by the capture—sometimes through methods strongly reminiscent of Gen. Jesup—of the more militant chiefs still at large—Wild Cat, Hospitaka, Halleck Tustenuggee—and writing off the problem of corralling the patriarchal Apiaca, or Sam Jones, and the more youthful Holata Micco, or Billy Bowlegs, as the rather futile job it had long been demonstrated to be. The Seminole now living in Florida are descended from the members of these two bands, mostly of the former, since a part of Billy Bowlegs' band, including Billy himself, were rounded up and shipped west as a result of the Third Seminole War, 1855–1858.

But another contribution to the liquidation of the war was a definitely changed policy toward the Negro element, including not only the Negroes of long standing in the tribe but the recent runaways, or "captured" Negroes, as well, foreshadowed by Jesup's prevention of the sale of captured Negroes by their Creek captors. Jesup's successors devoted themselves exclusively to getting the Indians and Negroes out of the everglades, out of the peninsula, and safely west of the Mississippi, and would on the whole rather ship a Negro west than return him to his legal owner, with the latter process involving the danger of alarming other Negroes who would

25. Van Ness, Maj. W. P., "An incident of the Seminole War," *Journal of the Military Service Institute of the United States,* vol. 1 (1912), pp. 267–271.

not only refuse to surrender themselves, but also influence the Negroes in general, and Indians as well, to stay out. The sensible theory developed among army officers that if a Negro didn't really want to be returned to his master—if he did, they would, of course, be glad to be of service—the quicker he was put on a steamboat for New Orleans and the Indian Territory, the better....

...The long struggle of the Negroes had not been entirely in vain. The Indian Negroes had again conclusively maintained the freedom which they or their ancestors had won first by flight and had then defended by force of arms against raids by Georgia borderers and in the First Seminole War; had they not thus demonstrated their mettle, but come passively in for transportation to the west, there is little doubt that many of them would have been enslaved. The slave raids against Negroes living among the Indians in West Florida, shortly before the outbreak of the Seminole War, are an indication of what the others might have expected, once they were made accessible to white aggression. Many, probably most, of the slaves who joined the Seminole at the outbreak of the war had been captured, through the double-dealing and treachery of Gen. Jesup and the perfidy of a few of the Indian chiefs, but those Negroes with both the initiative to join the Seminole in the first place and the courage, intelligence, tenacity, and good fortune to hold out until the third year of the war, i.e., about the middle of 1838, won their freedom, through being classified as "slaves" of the Indians, and were shipped to the Indian Territory along with the refugees of longer standing.

The participation of the Florida slaves in the Seminole War cannot, therefore, properly be disregarded. Hundreds, it is now known, seized the opportunity presented by the outbreak of the war to join the hostile Seminole Indians and Negroes. Those properly qualified by age and sex, strength and spirit, fought bravely and desperately at the side of Indian and Indian Negro, sometimes rising to positions of leadership. Others did good service behind the lines, collecting information and obtaining supplies for transmission to the hostiles. Free Negroes, with less to gain and more to lose than any others, nevertheless participated, both in the field and behind the lines. Particularly noteworthy were those Indian Negroes and runaways who operated as spies and secret agents, stealthily passing from Seminole camp to plantation or city slave-quarters and back again, to obtain recruits, information, and supplies. The general atmosphere of discontent and brooding hostility produced by all these operations and prevailing behind the lines held by the supporters of the slave system was such that it kept a large part of the militia at home, to guard against any sudden outbreak, thus relieving the pressure against the Indians and Negroes actually in the field and contributing to the prevention of their utter defeat.

Thus a close tie of common resistance to exploitation and oppression united the Indian chief, Wild Cat, the Indian Negro, John Caesar, the runaway slave, Andrew Gay, and the free Negro, Joe Merritt, who may stand as representatives of many other less known or entirely unknown figures in a fight for freedom of a century ago.

Part IV
Nonwhites in a Volatile Nation, 1840–1865

Nonwhites in a Volatile Nation, 1840–1865

Violence, territorial expansion, and a burgeoning nonwhite population marked the twenty-five-year period from 1840 to 1865 and created racial antagonisms which were not abated by the Civil War. Perhaps the key to understanding the era is the incessant craving of whites for new land, much of which was occupied by nonwhites.

Numerous Mexicans were annexed along with their lands as a result of the war which the United States waged against them. The Treaty of Guadalupe Hidalgo (1848) stipulated that the United States must grant the rights of citizenship to the new inhabitants. However, white Americans were selective in honoring the terms of the treaty, and many Mexican-Americans were deprived of both land and civil rights. Soon Spanish was no longer accepted in the southwest as an official language. Even in New Mexico where they outnumbered white immigrants, Mexican-Americans were unable to resist the decline because whites controlled the appointed territorial government.

Most blacks in the United States were enslaved and white southerners wanted to expand their "peculiar institution" to new land. This longing for land had led to war with Mexico, and southern zeal for carving new states out of the conquered territory became a major cause of the Civil War when northern abolitionists, both white and black, resisted the extension of slavery into the territories. Once the Civil War began, free blacks readily joined the union forces in an effort to end slavery, and those in bondage flocked to the lines of the union armies as they advanced southward. When the Civil War ended and the Thirteenth Amendment abolished legal slavery, blacks commenced their struggle for political, economic, and social equality.

Shortly after 1848 when the Chinese first entered the United States in response to dreams of wealth, discriminatory legislation was enacted to restrict their economic and legal rights and to deny them citizenship. The cultural heritage of the Chinese was attacked as well. For example, in 1855 San Franciscans enacted a "Pig Tail Ordinance" which provided that any Chinese man convicted of a crime should have his queue cut off. By the late 1850's, Chinese immigrants who entered the country as contract laborers frequently were forced to take jobs with western industries at miserly wages which kept them in debt bondage.

Although the southeastern Indians had already been removed from their lands by 1840, many of the Old Northwest tribes still suffered through the process of relocation. The Winnebagos, for example, were resettled seven different times in the thirty-five years before 1866, and other tribes also found the terms of treaties to be meaningless in defining their rights. Indians west of the Mississippi were relatively free from interference until the end of the Civil War when United States military power was turned against them, but even these tribes were not exempt from the intrusions of the landhungry Americans. When Stephen A. Douglas and other speculators wanted Kansas they pushed the Indians out, and in California, the Native American population was reduced by white-introduced disease and warfare from one hundred thousand in 1846 to thirty thousand in 1870. The Indians did not acquiesce in such depredations. Portents of the Plains Indian resistance which would plague western settlers for decades to come appeared when the Sioux of Minnesota revolted in 1862.

The westward movement, bringing with it the addition of the Mexican-American population, the issue of extending slavery into the territories, the importation of Chinese labor, and the dispossession and slaughter of the Indians created racial strife and left in its wake a residue of unsolved problems.

John C. Ewers,
"Blackfoot Camp Life"

Among the Indian nations populating the Great Plains as whites
pushed westward were the Blackfeet, who actually comprised
three tribes—the Piegan, the Kainah or Blood, and the Siksika or
Northern Blackfeet. The dominant military power of the
northwestern plains, Blackfeet roamed much of what is now the
state of Montana and the southern portions of the Canadian
provinces of Saskatchewan and Alberta. As did other Plains Indians,
the Blackfeet borrowed from the white invaders those devices
which could be readily adapted to their nomadic culture. For
example, the substitution of the horse for the dog enabled them
to transport more possessions and travel greater distances. It
also increased their effectiveness as hunters and fighters. To the
Plains Indians, the buffalo was of especial importance since most
of their food, clothing, shelter, and implements were derived
from that animal. In the following selection from The Blackfeet:
Raiders On the Northwestern Plains, John C. Ewers examines
various aspects of Blackfoot camp life.

Blackfoot Camp Life

John C. Ewers

In the middle of the nineteenth century Blackfoot life was a remarkable blend of traditional Indian customs modified by white influences. It was a way of life that would have been impossible without the European horse and the white man's trade goods. Nevertheless, Blackfoot economy was still based primarily upon buffalo hunting, as it had been in prehistoric times. Indeed, after American traders began to accept buffalo robes in trade, Blackfoot hunters had a greater incentive for killing buffalo than ever before. Then the buffalo not only furnished the Indians' subsistence but indirectly enabled them to obtain luxuries they never dreamed of before the coming of Napikwan [the white man]. Fortunately, buffalo were still very plentiful in the Blackfoot country. . . .

. . . Blackfoot hunting bands roamed over a vast area nearly twice the size of New England, extending from the North Saskatchewan River southward to the headwaters of the Missouri and from the Bearpaw Mountains westward to the Rockies.

The Blackfoot Indians' year was divided into four seasons of unequal length. The longest period was the one spent in winter camp. Each band wintered separately. In late October or early November the band chief selected a winter campsite in a broad river valley sheltered from winds and snow by the high, natural walls of the valley itself. The valley floor afforded grass for the horses. The river itself offered clear, cold drinking water, and the cottonwood groves bordering the stream provided firewood. As colder weather arrived in late November or early December men and women cut out the underbrush and some of the trees and moved their lodges into the timber. The standing trees served as windbreak and snow fence. Unless food became scarce or the wild grass for the horses was exhausted they remained in this locality throughout the winter.

Blackfoot winter dress was designed for comfort rather than for beauty. It bore little resemblance to the elaborately decorated costume we usually have in mind when we think of Plains Indians. When out-of-doors, men and boys wore buffalo-hide caps with ear flaps, buffalo robes with the hair next to the body or Hudson's Bay blanket coats, and hair-lined mittens and moccasins. Women and girls wore the same kind of moccasins, mittens, and headgear. Trade blankets or buffalo robes covered their undecorated dresses.

The Indians obtained their drinking water from holes chopped in the river ice. At these water holes the horses were watered three times daily. The horses were left to rustle for their food by pawing away the snow to the grass below. Some men fed their best horses the inner bark of cottonwood, which the Indians considered "better than oats." Others employed this supplemental feed only when the snow was too deep for the horses to rustle their own food. In some winters deep snows combined with very cold weather killed off many horses. In spite of everything their owners could do for them, the animals froze to death.

Throughout the winter beaver bundle owners kept primitive calendars of notched sticks, one notch representing each day, by which they could predict the approach of spring. The band chief carefully examined the development of embryos taken from buffalo cows killed in late winter hunts. When he saw that the unborn calves were beginning to develop hair, he knew spring was near. Before the river ice broke up, the beaver men held their ceremonies. When geese were seen flying north, all knew it was time to leave their winter camp. This was usually in late March or early April. After five or more months in one location the people were restless. They were glad to roam the plains again.

March was a difficult month during which the buffalo began to drift away from the sheltered river valleys. Unless the bands packed and followed the buffalo, they would have to subsist on small game or go hungry. Each band went its separate way in pursuit of buffalo. Buffalo calves were born in spring, between the breakup of winter camp and the annual May storm, a sudden and in some years heavy fall of snow which melted and disappeared almost overnight. The Indians killed calves for children's robes and soft skin sacks. The medicine pipe ceremony was performed after the first thunder was heard in spring, usually in April or May. Spring was also the season for making willow backrests to furnish tipis, constructing and repairing riding gear, and fashioning warm-weather clothing. Horses, thinned and weakened during the winter months, fattened and grew strong on the rich spring grasses. Toward the end of spring women dug bulbs, which provided a welcome change in diet after the long winter of eating meat and dried foods.

When buffalo bulls became prime in June, the scattered hunting bands began to gather for the tribal summer hunt. It required several weeks for these bands to assemble and for each to occupy its assigned segment of the tribal camp circle. Then began the organized summer hunt under the leadership of the tribal chief and the strict regulation of men's societies chosen to police the camp and hunt. This summer hunt provided cowhides for new tipi covers, meat, and most important of all, the sacrificial food for the sun dance—buffalo tongues. Only bull tongues were collected, and as many as three hundred might be needed. After the tongues were prepared and scouts had selected the site for the sun dance encampment, the entire tribe moved toward the site in four daily marches. These were dress parades on which the people wore their finest clothes, decorated their horses with their most elaborate trappings, and the men displayed their weapons and shields. Sarvis berries were ripe when the sun dance began, usually in August. Some eight or ten days were spent in the sun dance encampment. At the end of that period the tipis were taken down, the camp circle was dissolved, and the bands separated for their fall hunt. This summer season was the only time of year when all the bands of the tribe camped together in one great village. In this tribal encampment friendships between individuals of the different bands were formed, renewed, and strengthened, the men's societies held their ceremonies and competed against one another in games and races, young men courted girls of other bands, horses were bartered, painted lodges and sacred bundles were ceremonially transferred, successful warriors were honored, visitors from friendly tribes were feasted and showered with gifts, and the chiefs and headmen of the tribe met in council to discuss the economic, political, and military problems of the entire tribe and to make plans for the future. All these varied activities helped to strengthen feelings of tribal unity and solidarity among members of hunting bands who might not even see each other from one summer until the next.

Fall, when cows were prime, was the great buffalo-hunting season. Berries also were collected, dried, and mixed with meat to make pemmican. Each family tried to put up as much dried meat, berries, and pemmican as their winter needs required or their means of transportation would permit. The number of camp moves during this autumn season depended largely upon the availability of buffalo. The more plentiful the buffalo in the vicinity of a band camp, the less frequent were its movements. Even though this mobile period ended with the establishment of winter camp, men continued to hunt in the vicinity of the camp and women continued to prepare stores of food for winter and to dress buffalo robes for the trade until heavy snows and bitter cold weather restricted their activity.[1]

As the weather permitted, and when an accumulation of buffalo robes was available, the bands visited the trading posts. This trading season generally lasted from about the middle of November until the middle of April. In mid-April the traders began to press their winter's receipts in robes and furs into bales. By the end of the month they were ready to start loading their boats, and early in May their cargoes of robes and furs started on the long journey downriver to market.[2]

Thus the annual cycle of camp movements varied with the seasons. It was influenced not only by the availability of game and the ripening of wild plant foods, but also by the severity of the winter weather and the demands of the Indians' own ceremonial calendar. Through the cold months the bands were settled in their winter

1. Ewers, "Horse in Blackfoot Indian Culture," B.A.E. Bull. 159, 123–29.
2. McDonnell, "Fort Benton Journal," MHSC, Vol. X, 7–30.

camps. At that season they were no more nomadic than many tribes of the eastern forests who did not rely upon wandering buffalo herds for their subsistence. In their tribal sun dance encampment they obtained a brief rest between the most active hunting seasons in summer and fall.

Frequent camp movements during spring, summer, and fall required that Blackfoot Indian homes be portable and that their household furnishings and ceremonial equipment be easily and efficiently packaged. The head chief, with the advice of the band chiefs, determined the movements of the great tribal camp in summer. He sent his herald around the camp circle the night before a move was to be made to tell the people to be ready to get under way early the next morning. In the much smaller band camps during spring and fall the band chief consulted with other prominent men of his band before announcing a move.

On the morning camp movement was to get under way women were up and bustling around at dawn. They prepared the family breakfast, finished packing, and were on the move before eight o'clock. Most of the family belongings were packed the night before. They needed only to be tied in their assigned places on horses or travois. The principal task was that of taking down the lodge. Two or more experienced women could accomplish this in a few minutes. The buffalo-hide cover of an average-sized lodge weighed about one hundred pounds. It was carefully folded and tied in place between the horns of a pack saddle. The poles of such a lodge numbered nineteen. Each was about eighteen to twenty-two feet long and weighed a little less than twenty pounds. Women divided the lodge poles into bundles of about five poles each. They tied the poles of each bundle together by a rawhide cord threaded through a hole burned in each pole near its upper end and tied one bundle of poles on each side of a pack horse. Thus two horses were needed to drag the poles of an average-sized lodge.

Buffalo-robe bedding and willow backrests, the principal lodge furnishings, were packed on a horse travois. Dried meat, tallow, and pemmican were placed in rectangular, rawhide parfleches which were suspended over the horns of a saddle, one on each side of the pack horse. Berries and tobacco were packed in sacks made from the skins of unborn buffalo calves and placed in the side pockets of buffalo-hide saddlebags. Kettles were put into skin sacks and tied on top of the pack horses' loads. Tools and utensils were placed in rectangular rawhide cases, which usually were carried on the horse travois. Ceremonial equipment was carried in bundles on the travois or in fringed rawhide containers over the horns of the favorite wife's saddle.

Scouts rode well in advance of the moving caravan, on constant lookout for signs of game or enemies. The other active warriors rode on the flanks and in the rear of the moving camp, carrying their weapons. The medicine pipe owner and the chief or chiefs and their families led the main body. Other camp members fell in behind the chiefs in family groups with their travois, pack animals, riding horses, and loose horses. Older boys drove the loose horses. Babies rode on their mothers' backs in the folds of their mothers' buffalo robes. Toddlers often rode on the travois. When they tired of riding, they got off and ran for a while. Older children usually rode horseback, sometimes two or three of them on a horse.

At noon the chief halted the caravan for a short rest and lunch. This was a cold meal of prepared meat, pemmican, or dried plant foods, and water. Usually the day's march ended in the middle or late afternoon so there was ample time for the women to erect the lodges, unpack the horses, and prepare the evening meal before dark. The chief chose the campsite and selected the spot for his lodge. Only during tribal movements in summer was the camp circle formed. At the end of a day's march by a separate hunting band the families pitched their lodges around that of their chief in an uneven cluster. They did not scatter widely because of the danger of enemy attack.

Usually the Indians knew in advance if their night camp was to be made without wood or water. If wood was lacking, dried buffalo chips were collected. Dried grass was used for tinder. The grass was ignited by sparks made by striking a curved fire-steel against a piece of flint. Water was brought along in buffalo paunches to supply a dry camp. Horses and dogs were watered in basin-shaped troughs of rawhide. There was little difficulty in obtaining water in spring. At that season the water from melting snows collected in many depressions which dried out by summer time.

When the Indians had to cross deep streams or rivers on the march, they rolled up the sides of their lodge covers to form rude boats in which baggage and children were placed. Horse travois poles and tipi poles were lashed together to form crude rafts on which other baggage was ferried. Horses towed these improvised craft while men swam ahead with tow lines, guiding the way, and women pushed from behind. Horses whinnied, dogs yelped, and people shouted as the crossing was made. When the Indians reached the far side of the stream, they generally stopped for the day to dry their clothes and gear.

On a rainy morning the Indians usually did not try to move camp. If a heavy rain fell while the band was on the march, they generally stopped for the day. Other factors helped to determine both the speed of movement and the distance covered. Among them were the character of the terrain traversed (whether level or hilly, the number and sizes of the water courses to be crossed), the availability of game, fear of enemy raiding parties in the vicinity, and the desire to reach a trading post or a particular camping spot before nightfall.

A normal day's march was about ten to fifteen miles. This was fully twice the distance the prehistoric ancestors of the Blackfeet could have made on foot carrying their meager possessions on dog travois and the backs of their women. A horse packing two hundred pounds on its back or hauling three hundred pounds on the travois could move four times the load of a heavily burdened dog twice as far on a day's march. So, animal for animal, the horse was eight times more efficient than the dog as a burden bearer. The application of horse power to camp movement thus enabled the Blackfeet to accumulate more property and to move it faster and farther as well.

An average family of eight persons (including two grown males, three women, and three children) needed ten horses to move camp efficiently. They needed a horse to carry the lodge cover and its accessories; two horses to drag the lodge poles; two for packing meat, other food, and equipment; three horses to carry the women (at least two of which would drag travois); and two riding horses for the men. Each of the men would also need a buffalo horse. A young married couple with a baby or no children needed no more than five horses. However, a large family of more than five adults required fifteen to twenty or more horses.[3]

Nevertheless, there were many poor families among the Blackfeet who owned only one or two horses. Their poverty in horses caused

3. Ewers, "Horse in Blackfoot Indian Culture," B.A.E. Bull. 159, 129–39.

their standard of living to be well below that of the average family in their tribe at the time. Their possessions more nearly resembled those of the pre-horse Indians in quantity. Their lodges were small, covered with no more than six or seven buffalo hides, with short, light foundation poles. Their clothing, household utensils, and weapons were few and poor in quality. They owned no fancy dress clothes, no handsome riding gear. Their guns, if they owned any, were worn, broken, and repaired with rawhide cord. They had few if any buffalo robes to offer the traders.

At the other end of the Blackfoot economic and social ladder were the relatively few wealthy families—the owners of large horse herds. The fur trader, Charles Larpenteur, writing in 1860, aptly characterized the rich Indian:

It is a fine sight to see one of these big men among the Blackfeet, who has two or three lodges, five or six wives, twenty or thirty children, and fifty to a hundred horses; for his trade amounts to upward of $2,000 a year.[4]

The man of wealth and the members of his family dressed well. They owned several changes of clothing, including elaborately decorated garments to wear in dress parades, ceremonies, and feasts in honor of important visitors and on their own visits to other Indian camps or to the trading posts. They obtained the most attractive ornaments and best weapons from the traders' stock. They owned important and costly medicine bundles and showy and well-made riding gear. Their tipis were both large and handsomely furnished. As Larpenteur stated, some of them owned more than one tipi.

Wealth brought both opportunity and responsibility to the man who possessed it. The stingy rich man was despised by his less fortunate fellows. The generous man of wealth was beloved by them. If he was liberal in feasting and in giving away food and horses to the needy, if he lent horses to the poor for their use in hunting and moving camp, his fellow band members would want him for their chief—provided he also possessed a fine war record. James Doty described the Blackfoot chieftaincy thus in 1854:

4. *Forty Years a Fur Trader*, II, 401.

Every man who can acquire a large herd of horses, keep a good Lodge and make a large trade in Buffalo Robes is a chief, and he will maintain a persuasive influence over his people just so long as he continues wealthy, and ministers to the popular voice in directing the movements of the camp, leading war parties etc. Whenever he opposes his wishes to those of his band, it will desert him and turn to some chief more pliable.[5]

The hunting band, which was still the basic political unit among the Blackfeet, was probably a much more fluid unit than it had been in prehistoric times. In early times, when everyone stood literally and figuratively on an equal footing, the chiefs had no property to dispense. But in the middle of the nineteenth century poor families looked to their chief for charity. They changed their band allegiance if they believed they might better their economic condition as followers of a more liberal chief. Some of the larger bands had more than one chief. New bands were created when a rising leader and his followers broke away from an existing band. An older band might dissolve after the death of a prominent chief if there was no one who could take his place in the hearts of his followers. Even the names of bands were changed in honor of particular chiefs or in memory of some unusual happening to the band. As a result, contemporary and later estimates of the number of hunting bands in each of the three Blackfoot tribes in the middle of the nineteenth century vary widely. The tendency of later students was to list every band encountered as a separate one, whether or not they were all contemporaneous. It seems most probable that in mid-century the Piegans comprised about thirteen bands, averaging about twenty-five lodges and about two hundred souls per band. In the winter of 1869–70 General Sully listed fifteen Piegan bands and nine bands each in the Blood and North Blackfoot tribes. These bands ranged from ten to thirty-six lodges each. Their average size was twenty-four lodges.[6]

The most influential band chief became recognized as the head chief of his tribe. However, his rank was of little significance except during the period of the tribal encampment in summer. Even then

---

5. Doty to Isaac I. Stevens, December 20, 1854. Indian Office Records.

6. General Alfred Sully, Census of Blackfoot Indians, 1870, Indian Office Records.

his role was more that of chairman of the council of chiefs than of ruler of his people. Important decisions were reached by agreement in council after each chief had an opportunity to speak his mind.

The chiefs exercised little disciplinary power over their followers. In the summer tribal encampment, selected men's societies policed the camp. But throughout the greater part of the year, when the tribe was divided into separate hunting bands, tribal discipline simply did not exist. The individual who was wronged was expected to exact such punishment of the wrongdoer as he or his family was able to inflict. Not uncommonly, the criminal fled to another Blackfoot band or to a neighboring tribe. Theft customarily was followed by reclaiming of the stolen property. Murder was punished by the dead man's relatives, who usually took the life of the murderer. But if the murdered man was poor and the killer rich and powerful the matter might be ended by a payment of horses to the family of the deceased. Thus it was possible for a wealthy man literally to get away with murder, although he would not enhance his popularity by doing so....

Young men enjoyed remarkable freedom in their sexual life. They accosted girls while they were alone gathering wood or water on the outskirts of camp. They bragged of their conquests, particularly if they had had an affair with a married woman. Chastity before marriage was more an ideal than a reality for many girls. Yet a girl who earned a reputation for being too free with her favors might have to be satisfied with marrying a poor boy whose future prospects were equally poor....

Polygamy was common among the Blackfeet because it was a practical means of caring for the excess of women created by heavy war losses. Women outnumbered men by two or three to one. Possession of several wives was one of the distinguishing marks of the successful man. A few of the leading chiefs had ten or more wives. Probably more than half of the men had at least two. In these polygamous households the husband's favorite, his "sits-beside-me-wife," accompanied him to feasts and ceremonies and supervised the work of the other women in her husband's home. Cautious men tried to minimize the dangers of jealousy and friction at home by marrying sisters. A husband of an eldest sister could expect the younger ones to be offered to him as they reached marriageable age, although he did not have to accept them. Double-Victory-Calf-Robe had two elder sisters, both of them married to Iron Horn. One day her father said to her, "My son-in-law, Iron Horn, is very kind and good to us. You had better marry him and be with your sisters." Her family outfitted a travois, helped her mount the travois horse, and she rode over to Iron Horn's lodge. He accepted her as his third wife and gave horses to her father . . . .

In their late teens a group of young men banded together to purchase membership in the lowest of the graded men's societies at the tribal sun dance encampment. They selected a leader, who presented a pipe to the leader of the society. Each of the other youths gave pipes to other members of the society. If the pipes were accepted, the petitioners were expected to make other gifts of horses and valuable goods to those who relinquished their society membership to them and who taught them the ceremonial procedures of the organization. It was usual for societies to sell out to a group of younger men every four years.

There were seven of these age-graded men's societies among the Blackfeet in 1833. The youngest group was then the Mosquitos, the oldest the Buffalo Bulls. Two decades later the Bulls Society among the Piegans had become inactive on account of the death of many of its older members, but a new society, the Pigeons, or Doves, had been added to the bottom of the series.[7]

Because members of these societies belonged to different hunting bands, they were only active during the summer season when the tribal camp was organized. At that time the head chief called upon one or two of the societies, usually the younger of the mature groups, to police the camp and the tribal hunt. In the sun dance camp each society performed its peculiar ceremony. Collectively, the men's societies were known as the All-Comrades.[8]

There was a women's society among the Blood and Northern Blackfoot tribes which was unknown among the Piegans. Its members were wives of the most highly respected men in their tribes. Prior to the sun dance in summer, members of this Matoki society built a ceremonial lodge which resembled a buffalo corral, and on the final

7. Maximilian, Travels, II, 112–17.

8. Clark Wissler, "Societies and Dance Associations of the Blackfoot Indians." American Museum of Natural History Anthropological Papers, Vol. XI, Part 4, .361–450. Includes detailed description of specialized paraphernalia and ceremonies of each society.

day of their four-day ritual re-enacted the drive of buffalo into the corral. Some of the members wore buffalo headdresses and mimicked the actions of buffalo.[9]

The aged were no longer abandoned on the plains as had been the common lot of enfeebled old people before the Blackfeet acquired horses. If an old man or woman was too feeble to ride alone, he or she was carried on the A-shaped horse travois. If the head of a family knew he was about to die, he called his relatives together and told them how he wished his horses and other property divided among them. If he died without having made such a verbal will, the other people in camp made a run for his property as soon as they heard his relatives weeping and wailing. Men ran for his horses; women went for his household equipment. The men might take all his best horses and leave the poorest ones for his widow. Close relatives of the deceased, preoccupied with mourning his loss, made no attempt to prevent this raid on his property. Custom decreed that they should not do so. These raids were made with particular relish upon the property of a man of wealth who had had a reputation for miserliness during his lifetime. . . .

9. *Ibid.*, 430–35.

Raymond A. Bauer and Alice H. Bauer,
"Day to Day Resistance to Slavery"

*Slavery's apologists justified the "peculiar institution" by claiming
that blacks were contented in bondage and inherently unable
to cope with the intricacies of life in the United States without
direction from their white superiors. The whites' duty was
to use the paternalistic auspices of slavery to educate, civilize,
uplift, and Christianize the black slaves. However, as most astute
plantation owners knew, blacks hated slavery and demonstrated
their dislike by participating in revolts, running away from
plantations, murdering whites, and seizing any opportunities for
freedom. Hatred for the institution was also illustrated in more subtle
ways. Masking emotions with a smiling countenance, a bow, or
a "yes sir," slaves worked as slowly as possible, ruined implements,
set buildings on fire, and plotted vengeance against the slaveowner.
In the following article, Raymond Bauer and Alice Bauer
catalogue some of the many forms of "day to day resistance"
to the institution of slavery. Slaves were, as another historian
asserted, "a troublesome property."*

Day to Day Resistance to Slavery[1]

Raymond A. Bauer and Alice H. Bauer

The tradition that has grown up about Negro slavery is that the slaves were docile, well adapted to slavery, and reasonably content with their lot. . . .

This concept is gradually being changed as the study of slave revolts, and of the social tension caused by the constant threat of revolt progresses.[2] In answer to the question, " 'Are the masters afraid of insurrection?' (a slave) says, 'They live in constant fear upon this subject. The least unusual noise at night alarms them greatly. They cry out, 'What is that?' 'Are the boys all in'?"[3]

Abridged from Raymond A. Bauer and Alice H. Bauer, "Day to Day Resistance to Slavery," pp. 388–419. Copyright © by The Association for the Study of Negro Life and History, Inc. Published in *The Journal of Negro History*, XXVII (October 1942). Some footnotes have been renumbered.

1. We wish to express our appreciation to Professor M. J. Herskovits, under whose direction this research has been carried on.

2. Cf. Aptheker, Herbert, "American Negro Slave Revolts," *Science and Society*, 1:512–538, 1937; Wish, Harvey, "American Slave Insurrections before 1861," *Journal of Negro History*, 23:435–450, 1928; Wish, Harvey, "The Slave Insurrection Panic of 1856," *Journal of Southern History*, 5:206–222, 1939; see also Herskovits, M. J., *The Myth of the Negro Past*, pp. 99–105.

3. Clarke, Lewis, *Narratives of the Sufferings of Lewis and Milton Clarke*, Boston, 1846, p. 123.

Raymond A. Bauer and Alice H. Bauer

The purpose of this paper is to study a less spectacular aspect of slavery—the day to day resistance to slavery, since it is felt that such a study will throw some further light on the nature of the Negro's reaction to slavery. Our investigation has made it apparent that the Negroes not only were very discontented, but that they developed effective protest techniques in the form of indirect retaliation for their enslavement. . . .

The picture of the docile, contented Negro slave grew out of two lines of argument used in ante-bellum times. The pro-slavery faction contended that the slaves came of an inferior race, that they were happy and contented in their subordinate position, and that the dancing and singing Negro exemplified their assumption. Abolitionists, on the other hand, tended to depict the Negro slave as a passive instrument, a good and faithful worker exploited and beaten by a cruel master. As one reads the controversial literature on the slavery question, it soon becomes apparent that both sides presented the Negro as a docile creature; one side because it wished to prove that he was contented, the other because it wished to prove that he was grossly mistreated. Both conceptions have persisted to the present time. Writers who romanticize the "Old South" idealize the condition of the slaves, and make of them happy, willing servitors, while those who are concerned with furthering the interests of the Negroes are careful to avoid mention of any aggressive tendencies which might be used as a pretext for further suppressing the Negroes. . . .

The conceptual framework within which this paper is written is that the Negro slaves were forced into certain outward forms of compliance to slavery; that, except for the few who were able to escape to the North, the Negroes had to accept the institution of slavery and make their adjustments to that institution. The patterns of adjustment which we have found operative are: slowing up of work, destruction of property, malingering and self-mutilation. . . .

The Negroes were well aware that the work they did benefited only the master. "The slaves work and the planter gets the benefit of it."[4] "The conversation among the slaves was that they worked

4. Wm. Brown, an escaped slave; in: Benjamin Drew, *The Refugee*, Boston, 1856, p. 281.

hard and got no benefit, that the masters got it all."[5] It is thus not surprising that one finds many recurring comments that a slave did not do half a good day's work in a day. A northerner whom Lyell met in the South said:

> "Half the population of the south is employed in seeing that the other half do their work, and they who do work, accomplish half what they might do under a better system."[6]

An English visitor, with a very strong pro-slavery bias corroborates this:

> "The amount of work expected by the field hand will not be more than one half of what would be demanded of a white man; and even that will not be properly done unless he be constantly over-looked."[7] ...

Just how much of this was due to indifference and how much due to deliberate slowing up is hard to determine. Both factors most probably entered. A worker who has to devote himself to a dull task from which he can hope to gain nothing by exercising initiative soon slips into such a frame of mind that he does nothing more than go through the motions. His chief concern is to escape from the realities of his task and put it in the back of his mind as much as possible.

There is, indeed, a strong possibility that this behavior was a form of indirect aggression....

Certainly description after description emphasizes the mechanical plodding of the slave workers.

> "John Lamar wrote, 'My man Ned the carpenter is idle or nearly so at the plantation. He is fixing gates and, like the idle groom in Pickwick, trying to fool himself into the belief that he is doing something—He is an eye servant.' "[8] ...

5. Thomas Hedgebeth, a free Negro; in: Benjamin Drew, *The Refugee*, Boston, 1856, p. 276.

6. Lyell, Sir Charles, *A Second Visit to the United States of America*, New York, 1849, II, 72.

7. Ozanne, T. D., *The South as It Is*, London, 1863, pp. 165, 166.

8. Phillips, U. B., *American Negro Slavery*, New York, 1918, p. 192.

To what extent this reluctant labor was the rule may be appreciated when it is pointed out that a southern doctor classified it under the name *Dysaethesia Aethiopica* as a mental disease peculiar to Negroes. Olmsted quotes this Dr. Cartwright as follows:

> " 'From the careless movements of the individual affected with this complaint, they are apt to do much mischief, which appears as if intentional, but it is mostly owing to the stupidity of mind and insensibility of the nerves induced by the disease. Thus, they break, waste, and destroy everything they handle—abuse horses and cattle—tear, burn, or rend their own clothing, and, paying no attention to the rights of property, steal others to replace what they have destroyed. They wander about at night, and keep in a half nodding state by day. They slight their work—cut up corn, cotton and tobacco, when hoeing it, as if for pure mischief. They raise disturbances with their overseers, and among their fellow servants, without cause or motive, and seem to be insensible to pain when subjected to punishment.
>
> " '...The term "rascality" given to this disease by overseers, is founded on an erroneous hypothesis, and leads to an incorrect empirical treatment, which seldom or never cures it.' "[9]

There are only two possible interpretations of the doctor's statement. Either the slaves were so extraordinarily lazy that they gave the appearance of being mentally diseased, or the doctor was describing cases of hebephrenic schizophrenia. Either situation is startling. The phenomenon was obviously widespread, and if it was actually a mental disease it certainly would indicate that Negroes did not become "easily adjusted to slavery."

Whatever the case, it is certain that the slaves consciously saved their energy. Olmsted, who always had his eye open for such incidents, reported:

> "The overseer rode among them, on a horse, carrying in his hand a raw-hide whip, constantly directing and encouraging them; but, as my companion and I, both, several times noticed, as often as he visited one line of the operations, the hands at the other end

9. Olmsted, F. L., *A Journey in the Seaboard Slave States*, New York, 1863, pp. 192, 193.

would discontinue their labor, until he turned to ride toward them again."[10]

The few statements on this point we have by ex-slaves seem to indicate that the slaves as a group made a general policy of not letting the master get the upper hand. . . .

Writer after writer, describing incidents in which slaves were compelled to assist in punishing other slaves states that they did so with the greatest of reluctance.

> "The hands stood still;—they knew Randall—and they knew him also to be a powerful man, and were afraid to grapple with him. As soon as Cook had ordered the men to seize him, Randall turned to them, and said—'Boys, you all know me; you know that I can handle any three of you, and the man that lays hands on me shall die. This white man can't whip me himself, and therefore he has called you to help him.' The overseer was unable to prevail upon them to seize and secure Randall, and finally ordered them all to go to their work together."[11]

In some cases it was noted that the slave resisting punishment took pains not to treat his fellows with any more than the absolute minimum of violence.

With such demonstrations of solidarity among the slaves it is not surprising to find a slave telling of how he and his fellows "captured" the institution of the driver. The slave Solomon Northrup was such a driver. His task was to whip the other slaves in order to make them work.

> " 'Practice makes perfect,' truly; and during eight years' experience as a driver I learned to handle the whip with marvelous dexterity and precision, throwing the lash within a hair's breadth of the back, the ear, the nose without, however, touching either of them. If Epps was observed at a distance, or we had reason to apprehend

---

10. *Ibid.*, p. 388.

11. Brown, W. W., *Life of Williams Welles Brown, A Fugitive Slave*, Boston, 1848, p. 18. See also Williams, James, *Narratives of James Williams*, Boston, 1838, pp. 56, 62, 65.

he was sneaking somewhere in the vicinity, I would commence plying the lash vigorously, when, according to arrangement, they would squirm and screech as if in agony, although not one of them had in fact been grazed. Patsey would take occasion, if he made his appearance presently, to mumble in his hearing some complaints that Platt was whipping them the whole time, and Uncle Abram, with an appearance of honesty peculiar to himself would declare roundly I had just whipped them worse than General Jackson whipped the enemy at New Orleans."[12]

The amount of slowing up of labor by the slaves must, in the aggregate, have caused a tremendous financial loss to plantation owners. The only way we have of estimating it quantitatively is through comparison of the work done in different plantations and under different systems of labor. The statement is frequently made that production on a plantation varied more than 100% from time to time. Comparison in the output of slaves in different parts of the South also showed variations of over 100%. Most significant is the improvement in output obtained under the task, whereby the slaves were given a specific task to fulfill for their day's work, any time left over being their own. . . .

The slaves were well aware of their economic value, and used it to good advantage. The skilled laborers among the slaves knew their worth, and frequently rebelled against unsatisfactory work situations. Slaves who were hired out would run away from the masters who had hired them, and then either return home, or remain in hiding until they felt like returning to work.

"The slave, if he is indisposed to work, and especially if he is not treated well, or does not like the master who has hired him, will sham sickness—even make himself sick or lame—that he need not work. But a more serious loss frequently arises, when the slave, thinking he is worked too hard, or being angered by punishment or unkind treatment, 'getting the sulks,' takes to 'the swamp,' and comes back when he has a mind to. Often this will not be till the year is up for which he is engaged, when he will return to his owner, who, glad to find his property safe, and that it has not died

12. Northrup, Solomon, *Twelve Years a Slave*, 1853, pp. 226, 227.

in the swamp, or gone to Canada, forgets to punish him, and immediately sends him for another year to a new master."[13] ...

Even the threat of a whipping did not deter such slaves from running off for a time when they were displeased.... Some of the resistance took on the aspects of organized strikes.

"Occasionally, however, a squad would strike in a body as a protest against severities. An episode of this sort was recounted in a letter of a Georgia overseer to his absent employer: 'Sir: I write you a few lines in order to let you know that six of your hands has left the plantation—every man but Jack. They displeased me with their work and I give some of them a few lashes, Tom with the rest. On Wednesday morning they were missing. I think they are lying out until they can see you or your Uncle Jack.' The slaves could not negotiate directly at such a time, but while they lay in the woods they might make overtures to the overseer through slaves on a neighboring plantation as to terms upon which they would return to work, or they might await their master's posthaste arrival and appeal to him for a redress of grievances. Humble as their demeanor might be, their power of renewing the pressure by repeating their act could not be ignored."[14] ...

The indifference of the slaves to the welfare of the masters extended itself to a complete contempt for property values. The slaves were so careless with tools that they were equipped with special tools, more clumsy than ordinary ones.

"The 'nigger hoe' was first introduced into Virginia as a substitute for the plow, in breaking up the soil. The law fixes its weight at four pounds,—as heavy as the woodman's axe. It is still used, not only in Virginia, but in Georgia and the Carolinas. The planters tell us, as the reason for its use, that the negroes would break a Yankee hoe in pieces on the first root, or stone that might be in their way. An instructive commentary on the difference between free and slave labor!"[15]

13. Olmsted, *op. cit.*, pp. 100, 101.
14. Phillips, U. B., *American Negro Slavery*, pp. 303, 304.
15. Parson, C. G., *Inside View of Slavery*, Boston, 1853, p. 94.

Not only tools but livestock suffered from the mistreatment by the slaves. Olmsted found not only the "nigger hoe" but even discovered that mules were substituted for horses because horses could not stand up under the treatment of the slaves. . . .

Redpath verifies Olmsted's statement—by telling how he saw slaves treat stock. It is important to note that Redpath was a strong abolitionist and most sympathetic toward the slaves.

"He rode the near horse, and held a heavy cowhide in his hand, with which from time to time he lashed the leaders, as barbarous drivers lash oxen when at work. Whenever we came to a hill, especially if it was very steep, he dismounted, lashed the horses with all his strength, varying his performances by picking up stones, none of them smaller than half a brick, and throwing them with all his force, at the horses' legs. He seldom missed.

"The wagon was laden with two tons of plaster in sacks.

"This is a fair specimen of the style in which Negroes treat stocks."[16] . . .

In the Sea Islands off the coast of Georgia, Kemble reported that the slaves started immense fires, destroying large sections of woods through carelessness or maliciousness. . . .

The slaves on Lewis' West Indies plantation let cattle get into one of his best cane-pieces because they neglected to guard them, being more interested in a dance which was going on. They were fully aware that the cattle were ruining the sugar cane, but kept right on singing and dancing. Lewis was able to get only a handful of house servants to drive the cattle out of the cane, and that not until the cane-piece was ruined.[17]

One tobacco planter complained that his slaves would cut the young plants indiscriminately unless they were watched. When it became late in the season and there was need of haste to avoid frost they would work only the thickest, leaving the sparser ones untouched.[18] Another planter said that he could cultivate only the

16. Redpath, James, *The Roving Editor: or, Talks with Slaves in the Southern States*, New York, 1859, p. 241.

17. Lewis, M. G., *Journal of a West Indian Proprietor, 1815–1817*, London, 1929, p. 267.

18. Phillips, U. B., *Plantation and Frontier Documents, 1649–1863*, Cleveland, 1909, p. 34.

poorer grades of tobacco because the slaves would not give necessary attention to the finer sort of plants.[19] An English visitor said:

> "The kitchens and out-offices are always at the distance of several yards from the principal dwelling. This is done as well to guard against the house-Negroes through carelessness setting the houses on fire, for they generally sit over it half the night, as to keep out their noise." (sic.)[20] . . .

But not only did the Negro slaves refuse to work, and not only did they destroy property, but they even made it impossible for planters to introduce new work techniques by feigning clumsiness. They prevented the introduction of the plow in this way on many plantations.[21] . . .

Malingering was a well-known phenomenon throughout the slave states.[22] The purpose of feigning illness was generally to avoid work, although occasionally a slave who was being sold would feign a disability either to avoid being sold to an undesirable master, or to lower his purchase price so as to obtain revenge on a former master. The women occasionally pretended to be pregnant, because pregnant women were given lighter work assignments and were allowed extra rations of food.

In a situation such as this in which physical disability was an advantage, one would expect much malingering. One might also expect to find functional mental disorders, hysterical disorders which would get one out of work. . . .

Of the extent to which illness was feigned there can, however, be

19. Olmsted, F. L., *A Journey in the Seaboard Slave States*, p. 91.

20. Hanson, C. W., *The Stranger in America*, London, 1807, p. 357.

21. Olmsted, *op. cit.*, pp. 481–484.

22. Since this paper was written a significant contribution has appeared which throws a new light on the subject of slave illness. (Felice Swados, "Negro Health on the Ante Bellum Plantations," *Bulletin of the History of Medicine*, vol. x, no. 3, October, 1941.) Though Swados demonstrated that the rate of actual sickness among the Negroes was very high, she leaves some doubt as to what proportion of sickness was feigned. For instance, in a footnote (p. 472) she refers to Sydnor's compilations of the records of sickness on several plantations as indications of the extent of actual sickness, even going so far as to note that on one plantation most of the sickness occurred during the picking season. Sydnor, himself, indicates that he believes that these records demonstrate that a great deal of the sickness was feigned.

little doubt. Some of the feigning was quite obvious, and one might wonder why such flagrant abuses were tolerated. The important thing to remember is that a slave was an important economic investment. Most slave owners sooner or later found out that it was more profitable to give the slave the benefit of the doubt. A sick slave driven to work might very well die.

... The masters were always suspicious of the sick slaves, so that slaves who were moderately sick accentuated their symptoms in order to make out a convincing case. . . .

Fortunately in this field we have some quantitative estimates which enable us to appreciate fully the extent of these practices. Sydnor has digested the records of sickness on various plantations. From the Wheeles plantation records he found that of 1,429 working days 179 were lost on account of sickness, a ratio of almost one to seven. On the Bowles' plantation, in one year 159½ days were missed on account of sickness but only five days were on Sundays. This is a recurrent pattern, everybody sick on Saturday, and scarcely anybody sick on Sunday. On the Leigh plantation, where thirty persons were working there were 398 days of sickness. In examining this record Sydnor discovered that the rate of sickness was greatest at the times of the year when there was the most work to be done.[23] Olmsted says that he never visited a plantation on which twenty Negroes were employed where he did not find one or more not at work on some trivial pretext.[24] . . .

Pretending to be pregnant was a type of escape in a class by itself, since the fraud must inevitably have been discovered. This in itself may give us some insight into the Negroes' attitude toward the relative advantages of escaping work and of escaping punishment. Just as the slave who ran off into the woods for a temporary relief from work, the pseudo-pregnant woman must have realized in advance that she would inevitably be punished. . . .

One woman sought to escape from the consequences of her fraud. The results were quite tragic.

"A young slave woman, Becky by name, had given pregnancy as the reason for a continued slackness in her work. Her master became skeptical and gave notice that she was to be examined and

23. Sydnor, C. S., *Slavery in Mississippi*, New York, 1933. pp. 45 ff.
24. Olmsted, F. L., *A Journey in the Seaboard Slave States*, p. 187.

might expect the whip in case her excuse were not substantiated. Two days afterwards a Negro midwife announced that Becky's baby had been born; but at the same time a neighboring planter began a search for a child nine months old which was missing from his quarter. This child was found in Becky's cabin, with its two teeth pulled and the tip of its navel cut off. It died; and Becky was convicted only of manslaughter."[25] ...

The most effective means of retaliation against an unpopular master which the slave had at his command was by feigning disability on the auction block. How often this was done we do not know, but Phillips accepts it as a recognized pattern.

"Those on the block often times praised their own strength and talents, for it was a matter of pride to fetch high prices. On the other hand if a slave should bear a grudge against his seller, or should hope to be bought only by someone who would expect but light service he might pretend a disability though he had it not."[26] ...

The strength of Negro resistance to slavery becomes apparent in the extent to which the slaves mutilated themselves in their efforts to escape work. A girl on Lewis' plantation who had been injured tied pack thread around her wounds when they started to heal and then rubbed dirt in them. In her anxiety to avoid work she gave herself a very serious infection.[27] But this action was mild compared to that of others.

"General Leslie Coombs, of Lexington, owned a man named Ennis, a house carpenter. He had bargained with a slave-trader to take him and carry him down the river. Ennis was determined not to go. He took a broadaxe and cut one hand off; then contrived to lift the axe, with his arm pressing it to his body, and let it fall upon the other, cutting off the ends of the fingers.[28]

25. Phillips, U. B., *American Negro Slavery*, p. 436.
26. Phillips, U. B., *American Negro Slavery*, p. 199.
27. Lewis, *op. cit.*, p. 168.
28. Clarke, *op. cit.*, p. 125.

" 'But some on 'em would rather be shot then be took, sir,' he added simply.

"A farmer living near a swamp confirmed this account, and said he knew of three or four being shot on one day."[29]

Planters had much trouble with slaves fresh from Africa, the new slaves committing suicide in great numbers. Ebo landing in the Sea Islands was the site of the mass suicide of Ebo slaves who simply walked in a body into the ocean and drowned themselves. A planter writing on the handling of slaves mentions the difficulty of adjusting the Africans to slavery. He advocates mixing them in with seasoned slaves.

"It too often happens that poor masters, who have no other slaves or are too greedy, require hard labor of these fresh negroes, exhaust them quickly, lose them by sickness and more often by grief. Often they hasten their own death; some wound themselves, others stifle themselves by drawing in the tongue so as to close the breathing passage, others take poison, or flee and perish of misery and hunger."[30]

The one problem of Negro resistance to slavery which is most enticing is that of the attitude of slave mothers toward their children. There are frequent references in the literature to Negro women who boasted about the number of "niggers they hade for the massah," but breeding was probably quite secondary to sex activity. It would be interesting to discover the motives behind this apparent pleasure in presenting babies to the master. Some of the women may have been sincere in their pride. What makes this problem peculiarly important is the presence of much indirect evidence that, the Negro mothers either had no affection for their children, or did not want them to be raised as slaves.

We know quite well that African Negroes are (at least reasonably) able to take care of their children, and that the slave women efficiently tended the children of the plantation mistress. Yet one runs across comment after comment that the Negro mothers were ignorant, and

29. Olmsted, F. L., A Journey in the Seaboard Slave States, p. 160.
30. Phillips, U. B., Plantation and Frontier Documents, II, p. 31.

careless, and did not know how to care for their own offspring. Typical of such statements is this:

> "The Negro mothers are often so ignorant and indolent, that they cannot be trusted to keep awake and administer medicine to their own children; so that the mistress has often to sit up all night with a sick Negro child."[31]

Guion Johnson states that plantation owners in the Sea Islands offered the mothers rewards to take good care of their children. They were paid for those who survived the first year! This at least would indicate that there was something to be desired in their attitude toward their children.

Occasionally one runs across a reference to a slave mother killing her child, but the statements are almost invariably incomplete....

Several cases, where it was certain that parents killed their children to keep them from slavery, have been described. They are important enough to be given in detail.

> "Of all the cases of slave rendition, the saddest and probably the most circulated at the time was that of Margaret Garner. Winter was the best time for flight across the Ohio River, for when it was frozen over the difficulties of crossing were fewer. Simeon Garner, with his wife Margaret and two children, fled from slavery in Kentucky during the cold winter of 1856 and, after crossing the frozen stream at night, made their ways to the house of a free Negro in Cincinnati.
>
> "Quickly tracing the fugitive Negroes to their hideout in Cincinnati, the armed pursuers, after some resistance, broke down the door and entered the house. There they found Margaret, the mother, who, preferring death to slavery for her children, had striven to take their lives, and one child lay dead on the floor. The case was immediately brought into court, where despite the efforts made by sympathetic whites, rendition was ordered. On their return to slavery, Margaret in despair attempted to drown herself and child by jumping into the river but even the deliverance of death was denied her, for she was recovered and soon thereafter

31. Lyell, *op. cit.*, p. 264.

sold to a trader who took her to the cotton fields of the Far South."[32]

"Not only were slaves known to take the lives of their masters or overseers, but they were now and then charged with the murder of their own children, sometimes to prevent them from growing up in bondage. In Covington a father and mother, shut up in a slave barracoon and doomed to the southern market, 'when there was no eye to pity them and no arm to save,' did by mutual agreement 'send the souls of their children to Heaven rather than have them descend to the hell of slavery,' and then both parents committed suicide."[33]

" 'Take off your shoes, Sylva,' said Mrs. A., 'and let this gentleman see your feet.'
" 'I don't want to,' said Sylva.
" 'But I want you to,' said her mistress.
" 'I don't care if you do,' replied Sylva sullenly.
" 'You must,' said the mistress firmly.
"The fear of punishment impelled her to remove the shoes. Four toes on one foot, and two on the other were wanting! 'There!' said the mistress, 'my husband, who learned the blacksmith's trade for the purpose of teaching it to the slaves, to increase their market value, has, with his own hands, pounded off and wrung off all those toes, when insane with passion. And it was only last week that he thought Sylva was saucy to me, and he gave her thirty lashes with the horse whip. She was so old that I could not bear to see it, and I left the house.
" 'Sylva says,' Mrs. A. continued, 'that she has been the mother of thirteen children, every one of whom she has destroyed with her own hands, in their infancy, rather than have them suffer slavery'!"[34]

The patterns of resistance to slavery studied in this paper are: (1) deliberate slowing up of work; (2) destruction of property, and indifferent work; (3) feigning illness and pregnancy; (4) injuring one's

---

32. Coleman, J. W., *Slavery Times in Kentucky*, Chapel Hill, N. C., 1940, p. 208.
33. *Ibid.*, p. 269.
34. Parson, C. G., *op. cit.*, p. 212.

self; (5) suicide; (6) a possibility that a significant number of slave mothers killed their children. . . .

The material presented here suggests the need for a reconsideration of the concept of the Negro's easy adjustment to slavery. He was not a cheerful, efficient worker, as has been assumed. Rather, he was frequently rebellious, and almost always sullen, as any person faced with a disagreeable situation from which he cannot escape will normally be. Nor, can the belief that racial inferiority is responsible for inefficient workmanship on his part be supported. For such deficiencies of his workmanship as he manifested, or, indeed, may still be manifested, are seen to be explainable in terms that are in no sense to be couched in the conventional mold of inherent racial differences.

Although Mexican-Americans today constitute a population in the
southwestern United States of something over four million, they
are still considered by the Anglo majority to be an inconsequential
and exploitable element of society. Carey McWilliams, in " 'Not
Counting Mexicans,' " points out that this attitude is rooted in well
over a century of racial and cultural conflict. White Americans,
pursuing the spirit of "manifest destiny," forged relentlessly
westward during the eighteenth and nineteenth centuries and in the
process clashed with any peoples who impeded their march.
By the 1830s, a rupture was imminent with Mexico as Anglo
settlers gained numerical supremacy in Texas. Racial and cultural
differences helped to promote the rift. The Anglos were white, Protestant, English-speaking proponents of slavery. The Mexican
inhabitants were darker-skinned, Catholic, Spanish-speaking
opponents of slavery. McWilliams describes the events which
followed—the Texas Revolution, the Mexican-American War,
the disputes over slavery, and the Cortina Affair—as the genesis for
the tense and bitter feelings of today.

'Not Counting Mexicans'

Carey McWilliams

When asked how many notches he had on his gun, King Fisher, the famous Texas gunman, once replied: "Thirty-seven—not counting Mexicans." This casual phrase, with its drawling understatement, epitomizes a large chapter in Anglo-Hispano relations in the Southwest. People fail to count the non-essential, the things and persons that exist only on sufferance; whose life tenure is easily revocable. The notion that Mexicans are interlopers who are never to be counted in any reckoning dies but slowly in the Southwest. To this day Mexicans do not figure in the social calculations of those who rule the border states. As I write these lines [1948], the Mexican consul-general in Los Angeles has just entered a vigorous protest against the insulting behavior of custom inspectors at the municipal airport.

A majority of the present-day residents of the Southwest are not familiar with the malignant conflict of cultures which has raged in the borderlands for more than a century. Blinded by cultural myths, they have failed to correlate the major events in a pattern of conflict which has prevailed from Brownsville to Los Angeles since 1846. Once this correlation is made, it becomes quite apparent that the Mexican-

Carey McWilliams, " 'Not Counting Mexicans'," *North from Mexico: The Spanish-Speaking People of the United States* (New York: Greenwood Press, 1968), pp. 98–108. Copyright © 1948, reprinted by permission of the author.

American War was merely an incident in a conflict which arose some years before and survived long after the Treaty of Guadalupe Hidalgo. It is only within the framework of this age-old conflict that it is possible to understand the pattern of Anglo-Hispano cultural relations in the Southwest today. In summarizing the history of this conflict, one necessarily starts with Texas, for there the first blood was shed.

1. Los Diablos Tejanos

In Texas the Spanish-Mexican settlements were directly in the path of Anglo-American expansion. Unlike the rest of the borderlands, Texas was not separated from the centers of Anglo-American population by mountain ranges and desert wastes; geographically it invited invasion. In a series of belts or strips, its rich alluvial plains stretched from the plateaus to the gulf. The rivers that marked these belts could be crossed, at all seasons, at almost any point, without much trouble. On the other hand, between the most southerly settlements in Texas and those in Mexico, there was, as Dr. Samuel Harman Lowrie has pointed out, "a great expanse of semi-arid land which at that time served as a more or less natural, though temporary barrier to the effective extension of Mexican influence and control." Texas was 1,200 miles removed from its capital, Mexico City.

By 1834 the Anglo-Americans outnumbered the Mexicans in Texas: thirty thousand to five thousand. Most of the Mexicans were concentrated in the old Spanish towns or along the border, while the Anglo-Americans were to be found on the farms and ranches. Mexican townspeople had few opportunities for acculturation for they saw very little of the Anglo-Americans. From the outset, moreover, relations between the two peoples were clouded by the fear of war. The Anglo-Americans bore the brunt of Mexico's hostile distrust of the United States and were, in turn, encouraged to take an unfriendly attitude toward the natives by the unconcealed, aggressive designs of the jingoes in Washington.

As might have been expected, each group formed a highly unfavorable initial impression of the other. To the early American settlers, the Mexicans were lazy, shiftless, jealous, cowardly, bigoted, superstitious, backward, and immoral. To the Mexicans, on the other hand, the Texans were "los diablos Tejanos": arrogant, overbearing, aggressive, conniving, rude, unreliable, and dishonest. The first

Mexican ambassador to the United States had complained . . . of the "haughtiness of these republicans who will not allow themselves to look upon us as equals but merely as inferiors." Still another Mexican official had charged that the Americans in Texas considered themselves "superior to the rest of mankind, and look upon their republic as the only establishment upon earth founded upon a grand and solid basis." Full of brag, bluster, and spreadeagle chauvinism, the Americans of the 1800's were hardly the most tactful ambassadors of goodwill. The truth of the matter is that the border residents were not a credit to either group.

Under the most favorable circumstances, a reconciliation of the two cultures would have been difficult. The language barrier was, of course, a constant source of misunderstanding; neither group could communicate, for all practical purposes, with the other. The Mexicans knew almost nothing of local self-government, while the Americans, it was said, travelled with "their political constitutions in their pockets" and were forever "demanding their rights." Although tolerant of peonage, the Mexicans were strongly opposed to slavery. The Anglo-Americans, most of whom were from the Southern states, were vigorously pro-slavery. The Anglo-Americans were Protestants; the Mexicans were Catholic. Speaking of a Mexican, a Protestant missionary is said to have remarked: "He was a Catholic, but clean and honest." Both groups lacked familiarity with the existing Mexican laws, for there was no settled government in Texas. Anglo-Americans found it extremely difficult to respect the laws of Mexico in the absence of law-interpreting and law-enforcing agencies. Thus it was, as Dr. Lowrie writes, that "cultural differences gave rise to misconceptions and misunderstandings, misunderstandings to distrust, distrust to antagonism, and antagonism on a very considerable number of points made open conflict inevitable."

The first Anglo-Americans literally fought their way into Texas. While most of these early filibustering expeditions were defeated, they succeeded in laying waste to the country east and north of San Antonio. Both Mexicans and Americans were killed by these invading private armies. No sooner had the Mexicans driven out the filibusters, than the Comanches raided the entire stretch of country between the Nueces and the Rio Grande. According to one observer, the whole region was "depopulated, great numbers of stock were driven off, and the people took refuge in the towns on the Rio Grande." Preoccupied with revolutionary events in Spain and Mexico, the government could give little attention to the Texas settlements. After 1821, however, a measure of protection was provided against the devastating raids of the Comanches and many of the settlers moved back across the Rio Grande.

2. Alas! The Alamo

With the Texas Revolution came the embittering memories, for the Texans, of the slaughter of Anglo-Americans at the Alamo and Goliad; and, for the Mexicans, of the humiliating rout and massacre at San Jacinto. Prior bitternesses were now intensified a thousandfold. "Towards the Mexicans remaining within the limits of the Republic," writes Dr. Garrison, "the feeling of the Texans was scarcely better than towards the Indians." Memories dating from this period still poison relationships between Anglos and Hispanos in Texas. Some years ago a district judge told of how, as a child, he had heard an old man give an eye-witness account of the slaughter at the Alamo. "I never see a Mexican," he confessed, "without thinking of that." José Vasconcellos, the well-known Mexican educator and philosopher, tells in his autobiography of how these same memories poisoned his boyhood in Eagle Pass. After the Texas Revolution, as Erna Fergusson has pointed out, "Texans could not get it out of their heads that their manifest destiny was to kill Mexicans and take over Mexico."

Throughout the decade of the Texas Republic (1836–1846), the shooting war continued in "the Spanish country" south of the Nueces. Murder was matched by murder; raids by Texans were countered by raids from Mexico. Since a peace treaty was never negotiated, no boundaries could be fixed. Texas claimed to the Rio Grande, while Mexico insisted that its boundary rested on the Nueces. In the bloody zone between the two rivers an uninterrupted guerrilla warfare continued throughout the life of the Texas Republic. In 1839 General Don Antonio Canales launched a revolution on Texas soil against Santa Anna and raised the banner of the Republic of Rio Grande. Of the 600 men who rallied to his standard, 180 were Texans. Awakening to the fact that Texans were using his insurrection as a cover for an attack on Mexico, General Canales finally surrendered but not until his troops had fought several engagements along the border. At the head of a raiding party of five hundred men, General

Vásquez captured San Antonio in 1842 and held it for two days. These are but two of many similar episodes that occurred during the hectic life of the new republic.

Throughout the period of this border warfare, the Texas-Mexicans were caught between opposing forces. "When the Americans have gone there," explained a delegate at the Texas constitutional convention, "they have preyed upon the Mexicans; they have been necessarily compelled by force or otherwise to give up such property as they had. So vice versa, when the Mexicans have come in, they have been necessarily compelled to furnish them the means of support.... Since 1837 they [the Texas-Mexicans] have been preyed upon by their own countrymen as well as by ours." The Texans constantly suspected the Mexicans of inciting the Indians against them and every Indian raid provoked retaliation against the *Tejanos*. The Mexicans naturally regarded the Texas Revolution as American-inspired and the prelude to the conquest of Mexico.

However all Mexicans were not equally affected by this complex warfare. A sizable number of the upper-class settlers quickly became identified with the Texans. These Texanized Mexicans or "the good Mexicans" were called *Tejanos* and were invariably of the *rico* class. Two of the fifty signers of the Texas Declaration of Independence were native Mexicans and a third, born in Mexico, became the first vice-president of the republic. At a later date, Captain Refugio Benavides commanded a company of Texas-Mexicans which operated along the border against Mexican raiders and marauders.

3. The Mexican-American War

Provoked by the annexation of Texas in 1846, the Mexican-American War represented the culmination of three decades of cultural conflict in Texas. To the Mexicans, every incident in Texas from the filibustering raids to the Revolution of 1836 was regarded, in retrospect, as part of a deliberately planned scheme of conquest. To the Anglo-Americans, the war was "inevitable," having been provoked, in their eyes, by the stupidity and backwardness of the Mexican officials. Not only did Mexico forfeit an empire to the United States, but, ironically, none of the signers of the Treaty of Guadalupe Hidalgo realized that, nine days before the treaty was signed, gold had been discovered in California. That they had unknowingly ceded to the United States territories unbelievably rich in gold and silver—the hope of finding which had lured Coronado and De Oñate into the Southwest—must have added to the Mexicans' sense of bitterness and defeat.

Furthermore the way in which the United States fought the Mexican-American War added greatly to the heritage of hatred. A large part of our invading army was made up of volunteers who, by all accounts, were a disgrace to the American flag. General Winfield Scott readily admitted that they had "committed atrocities to make Heaven weep and every American of Christian morals blush for his country. Murder, robbery and rape of mothers and daughters in the presence of tied-up males of the families have been common all along the Rio Grande." Lieutenant George C. Meade, of later Civil War fame, said that the volunteers were "driving husbands out of houses and raping their wives. . . . They will fight as gallantly as any men, but they are a set of Goths and Vandals without discipline, making us a terror to innocent people."

How bitterly these outrages were resented is shown by a passage which Lloyd Lewis has culled from one of the Mexican newspapers of the period: "the horde of banditti, of drunkards, of fornicators . . . vandals vomited from hell, monsters who bid defiance to the laws of nature . . . shameless, daring, ignorant, ragged, bad-smelling, long-bearded men with hats turned up at the brim, thirsty with the desire to appropriate our riches and our beautiful damsels." The year 1844 had seen the rise of a Native American Party in the states and much anti-Catholic feeling found expression during the war. Mexicans charged that the volunteers had desecrated their churches, "sleeping in the niches devoted to the sacred dead . . . drinking out of holy vessels." Two hundred and fifty American troops, mostly of Catholic background, deserted and joined the Mexican army to form the San Patricio battalion. The barbarous manner in which eighty of these deserters were executed in San Angel, a suburb of Mexico City, was long cited by the Mexicans as further proof of Yankee cruelty.

Nothing was more galling to the Mexican officials who negotiated the treaty than the fact that they were compelled to assign, as it were, a large number of their countrymen to the Yankees. With great bitterness they protested that it was "not permissible to sell, as a flock of sheep, those deserving Mexicans." For many years after 1846, the Spanish-Americans left in the United States were known in Mexico as "our brothers who were sold." As late as 1943 maps were still used in Mexican schools which designated the old Spanish borderlands as "territory temporarily in the hands of the United States." It is to the great credit of the Mexican negotiators that the treaty contained the most explicit guarantees to protect the rights of these people, provisions for which they were more deeply concerned than they were over boundaries or indemnities. It should never be forgotten that, with the exception of the Indians, Mexicans are the only minority in the United States who were annexed by conquest; the only minority, Indians again excepted, whose rights were specifically safeguarded by treaty provision.

Just as the end of the Texas Revolution did not terminate hostilities in Texas, so the Treaty of Guadalupe Hidalgo failed to bring peace to the borderlands. Under the terms of the treaty, it became the obligation of the United States to police 180,000 Indians living in the territories which we acquired from Mexico. This obligation the United States failed to discharge for many years. Taking advantage of the confusion which prevailed, the Indians launched fierce raids on both Anglo and Hispano settlements, conducted marauding expeditions deep in Mexican territory, and cunningly exploited the hatred that had been engendered between Anglo and Hispano. The Anglos promptly attributed these raids to Mexican duplicity and instigation; the Hispanos as promptly charged them up to the malice or carelessness of the Americans. Hard-pressed on all sides, the Indians had come to live off the plunder seized in these raids which, with the confusion and demoralization which prevailed in Mexico, were conducted on a larger scale than ever before. It was not until about 1880 that the United States finally managed to bring the Indians of the Southwest under close police surveillance.

Nor were Indians the only troublemakers in the post-war decades. Between 1848 and 1853, various American filibustering expeditions violated Mexican territory in Sonora, Lower California, and at various points along the border. When word of the discovery of gold reached the Eastern states, swarms of emigrant gold-seekers passed along the southern routes to California, often travelling in Mexican territory without passports, and not infrequently helping themselves to Mexican food and livestock en route.

In 1850 José M. Carvajal organized a revolution in Mexico, sponsored by American merchants, which aimed at converting the State of

Tamaulipas into the Sierra Madre Republic. Carvajal was a Texan by birth who had been educated in Kentucky and Virginia. Backed by Richard King and Mifflin Kennedy, two of the great cattle-barons of south Texas, the Carvajal revolution was supported by bands of armed Texans who crossed the Rio Grande. The American ambassador reported that these raids, in which as many as five hundred Texans participated, had "awakened a feeling of intense prejudice against everything connected with American interest."

The fateful strip of territory between the Nueces and the Rio Grande once again became the home of numerous outlaw bands who preyed indiscriminately upon both Mexican and American settlers. In the face of these staggering blows,—filibustering expeditions, Indian raids, revolution, war, and constant guerrilla fighting,—the Mexicans in Texas constantly retreated and their retreat, of course, gave rise to the notion that their conquerors were pursuing a mandate of destiny. Major Emery, writing in 1859, said that the "white race" was "exterminating or crushing out the inferior race"; and an American soldier wrote home that "the Mexican, like the poor Indian, is doomed to retire before the more enterprising Anglo-Americans."

4. Slaves and Peons

As early as 1839 fairly large numbers of Negro slaves had escaped from their Texas owners by crossing the Rio Grande and a sizable colony of ex-slaves had sprung up in Matamoros. During the Civil War, the Texans suspected that native Mexicans were implicated in the flight of fugitive slaves, an accusation that found circumstantial confirmation in the known opposition of Mexicans to slavery (Mexico had sought to insert a provision in the treaty barring slavery forever from the territory ceded to the United States). "The possession of slaves in Western Texas," wrote Colonel Ford, "was rendered insecure owing to the contiguity of Mexico, and to the efforts of the Mexicans to induce them to run away. They assisted them in every way they could."

To some extent, the movement of Negro slaves across the border was matched by the flight of Mexican peons into Texas. According to Dr. Paul S. Taylor, some 2,812 servants with families numbering an additional 2,572 persons, escaped to Texas from Nuevo Leon and Coahuila in the period from 1848 to 1873. The loss in unpaid debts, which the flight of these peons represented, was estimated by the Mexican government to be in excess of $400,000.

In 1856 a Negro insurrectionary plot was uncovered in Colorado County. According to the Texans, the Negroes had planned to rebel, kill their masters, and, with the aid of native Mexicans, fight their way across the border. Without exception every Mexican in the county was "implicated" and over two hundred slaves were arrested and punished (two were whipped to death). Mexicans were ordered to leave Matagorda and Colorado counties immediately and in Uvalde they were forbidden to travel the roads without passes. "Anti-Mexican sentiment," writes Dr. Taylor, "based on the belief that the peons imperilled the institution of slavery, broke out in meetings which in Austin, Gonzales, and other towns, passed resolutions protesting against their employment. At Goliad the resolution declared that 'the continuance of the greaser or peon Mexicans as citizens among us is an intolerable nuisance and a grievance which calls loudly for redress'." As always, the circumstance that Mexicans were concentrated in the strip of territory immediately north of the border aroused the most dire forebodings.

The Negro insurrection was quickly followed by the Cart War which broke out in 1857. Prior to this time, Mexican ox-cart freighters had been hauling—between San Antonio and the coast and from San Antonio to Chihuahua—an annual cargo of goods and merchandise valued at several million dollars. The Cart War involved a systematic campaign on the part of Anglo-Americans to force Mexican freighters out of this lucrative business. For over a year, organized bands of Texans preyed on the Mexican freight trains, killing the drivers, stealing the merchandise, and generally disrupting the traffic. So tense did the situation become, with the Mexican ambassador filing one vigorous protest after the other, that federal troops were finally dispatched to protect the cartmen.

5. "Red Robber of the Rio Grande"
In the wake of the Cart War came the highly significant Cortina episode. Juan Nepomuceno Cortina—"the red robber of the Rio Grande"—was born near Brownsville. A blocky, powerfully built, red-bearded Mexican, Cortina came from a prominent and well-to-do family. Like so many Mexicans in Texas, he was a magnificent horse-

man. The Cortina War, which was to last a decade, started on July 13, 1859, when a deputy sheriff arrested a Mexican who had been a servant of the Cortina family. Contending that the arrest was merely another example of gringo arrogance, Cortina shot the deputy and freed the prisoner. On the morning of September twenty-eighth, Brownsville awoke to the cry of "*Viva Cortina! Viva Mexico! Maten los Gringos!*" as Cortina, at the head of an armed force, swept into the town, killed five Americans, released the *pelado* culprits from the jail, and plundered stores and shops. By 1860 Cortina had laid waste to the country from Brownsville to Rio Grande City—a distance of a hundred and fifty miles—and inland as far as Arroyo Colorado. Fifteen Americans and eight "friendly" Mexicans were killed in these raids, while Cortina is said to have lost a hundred or more of his men.

For fifteen years, Cortina was the scourge of the Lower Rio Grande Valley, defying capture, constantly eluding his pursuers. At one point in the Cortina War, Captain McNelly of the Texas Rangers crossed the Rio Grande, in defiance of orders, and gave Cortina's forces a severe defeat in a pitched battle at Las Cuevas. Incensed by these continued raids, the Texans burned the homes of all Mexicans suspected of being implicated or of giving aid and comfort to Cortina's forces. On his part, Cortina terrorized the Mexican residents and made short shrift of . . . informers. This continued terror naturally silenced the Mexicans—a circumstance which only confirmed the Texans' belief in their innate duplicity and treacherousness.

A real expert in border warfare, Cortina hoisted the Mexican flag in Texas, and, so it was said, often raised the American flag in Mexico. Both Texas Rangers and Mexican troops from Matamoros on more than one occasion met defeat at his hands. Although he was a bandit and a cattle-thief, there was unquestionably something of the Robin Hood about Cortina. He had become a desperado, so he said, because the Anglo-Americans had tried "to blacken, depreciate, and load with insults" the Mexican residents of Texas. In one of numerous manifestoes, he pointed out that "a multitude of lawyers" in Texas sought to rob the Mexicans of their lands. In particular, he charged that one Adolph Glavecke, a deputy sheriff, acting in collusion with certain lawyers, had spread terror among the Mexicans, threatening to hang them and to burn their homes unless they abandoned the country. "Our personal enemies," he said, "shall not possess our lands until they have fattened it with their gore." Major Heintzelman, on the border at the time, stated that after the Brownsville raid Cortina was a great hero in the eyes of the people. "He had defeated the gringo and his position was impregnable. He had the Mexican flag flying in his camp and numbers were flocking to his standard. He was the champion of his race—the man who would right the wrongs of the Mexicans and drive the hated Americans to the Nueces."

While some Mexicans undoubtedly sympathized with Cortina and gave him aid, it is also a matter of record that others, at great personal peril, joined in the fight to defeat him. Despite this fact, however, the Anglo-Texans believed that every Mexican along the border was in league with Cortina and would, if given a chance, "murder every white inhabitant." At the request of the American government, Díaz finally brought the Cortina War to a close in 1873 by making Cortina his prisoner; but, as Walter Prescott Webb has written, "the evil consequences lived on." . . .

Gunther Barth,
"Chinese Sojourners in the West: The Coming"

Beginning in 1848 the first Chinese immigrants to California
settled in the northern portion of the state at San Francisco
and near the gold fields. Gunther Barth describes the newcomers as
"Chinese Sojourners in the West," and indicates that these
were men who hoped to return to their homeland as wealthy and
respected individuals. He recounts the means by which Chinese
laborers were contracted, the types of the agreements which
were made for their labor, and the perils of the voyage to the
United States. Only a handful succeeded in returning to their
homeland; yet, immigration to the west coast increased, and within
a few years the Chinese comprised about 10 percent of the population
of California. The influx alarmed white Californians, who
feared the competition of Chinese labor and used threats, violence,
and legislation to bar the Orientals from the mines and other
potentially lucrative endeavors.

Chinese Sojourners in the West: The Coming

Gunther Barth

In the 1850's and 1860's, a wave of Chinese surged into California in pursuit of a dream. The newcomers envisioned making money to return to China with their savings for a life of ease, surrounded and honored by the families which their drudgery had sustained.[1] Their pursuit of this limited goal influenced their reception in America, excluded them from the privileges and obligations of other newcomers, and kept them apart from the flood of immigrants who entered the United States permanently. In America these Oriental sojourners became the docile subjects of bosses and headmen, still directed by the dictates of the Chinese world.

The Chinese overseas emigration to Southeast Asia provided the pattern for the Cantonese traffic to California. Unable to pay for their passage, the impoverished mass of travelers to the plantations, mines, and godowns of Malaysia relied on the credit-ticket system. They obtained their tickets on credit from Chinese merchants who furnished the transportation. In some cases, the creditors worked their debtors in any way that guaranteed a profitable return for their in-

Gunther Barth, "Chinese Sojourners in the West: The Coming," *Southern California Quarterly*, XLVI (1964), pp. 55–67. Reprinted by permission of the author. Notes appear at the end of the article.

vestment. In others, relatives of the travelers or their future employers, reimbursed the merchants for the passage. In return the newcomers labored until their debts were paid off and then were free to accumulate the modest fortune which had lured them across the sea. Only the completion of this task assured a return to their villages as respected men.[2]

The steady demand for docile laborers in Southeast Asia perpetuated the credit-ticket system. Dutch, English, and Spanish officials, realizing its immediate value for colonial development, tolerated its operation. At first sight, the arrangement by which passage money was advanced to laborers in Chinese ports and repaid by them out of their earnings overseas appeared an expedient and harmless device. In reality, the credit-ticket system camouflaged a world of debt bondage that turned indentured emigrants into slaves of their countrymen.

The extension of the credit-ticket system to the passage between Hongkong and San Francisco transplanted certain oppressive elements of the Chinese social structure to the United States. Although Californians opposed debt bondage, Chinese merchants successfully adjusted and masked the institution by utilizing district companies and kinship organizations as instruments of extra-legal control. The sojourners' loyalty to their families in the villages of the Pearl River Delta served to enforce the creditors' hold over the indentured emigrants. A review of the mode of coming discloses the outlines of a world of suppression and points to a source of future strife between Chinese and Americans. The details of the passage reveal the incipient control system: its transfer to the United States through the transport of indentured emigrants to California.

In addition to indentured emigrants, two other types of emigrants stood out among Chinese sojourners to Southeast Asia: contract laborers and coolies. In the contract system, foreign importers and Chinese middlemen played the principal role. They hired laborers to fill the specific demand for Chinese workers in Malaysia and America. In contrast to the credit-ticket system upheld by debt bondage, this labor system was based on a service contract. The coolie traffic to the West Indies, Latin America, and the Indian Archipelago produced the extreme form of the contract system in the middle of the nineteenth century.[3] Force alone sustained it. Kidnapped or decoyed into barracoons, the coolie was virtually sold into service. The term which originally designated a hired laborer soon came to describe any cheap worker who was pressed into and kept in service by coercion.

Indentured emigrants and contract laborers endured the hardships of coolies although they fell into their creditors' or contractors' clutches at their own volition. They were but one step removed from the despotism of the coolie trade. The nefarious traffic stimulated compassion for its victims and an increasing urge for control by western powers. The oppressive nature of the contract labor system and the subtle tyranny of the credit-ticket system escaped observers whose awareness was already blunted by the coolie trade's cruelty.[4] The three different types of labor represented mere variations on the basic theme of all these modes of Chinese emigration. They disguised the enslaved nature of the indentured emigrants, contract laborers, and coolies.

The adoption of the system of indentured emigrants to the western scene required modifications. These changes resulted from the dictates of geography, the conditions of California, and the objections of Americans to forms of labor resembling bondage or slavery. In March, 1852, the San Francisco *Alta California* referred to the movement of Chinese indentured emigrants into the Indian Archipelago as the prototype for the traffic to California. The newcomers at San Francisco, the paper explained, "had either contracted with wealthy Chinese at home to labor at the mines . . . , or had agreed on certain rates per month with the foreigners who brought them." But the ease with which "all contracts could be set aside, the temptation of the mines, and the impossibility of coercion, caused . . . these contracts to be broken with severe loss to the holders."[5] One year earlier, six Chinese laborers "who were under contract in consideration of a free passage," had demonstrated the weakness of the contract system in the United States. When they ran away to the mines, the contractor failed to get warrants for their arrest. Since the "offence was not cognizable by a criminal tribunal," the court recommended that he "obtain his remedy in a civil suit."[6]

The bulk of the Chinese emigration to California consequently depended on the credit-ticket system and its instruments of debtor control. Chinese brokers, merchants at San Francisco or at Hongkong, paid the expenses of the travelers. The emigrants remained under their supervision until these debts were paid off. To facilitate a speedy repayment, the Chinese merchants in California employed the laborers in their own enterprises or sold the lien on the emigrants' services to other employers.[7] Western sailing vessels substituted for Chinese junks, while district companies and kinship organizations functioned as extra-legal controls over the indentured emigrants in a country where courts and customs failed to support contract labor. During their sojourn, the majority of the emigrants rarely left the narrow confines of the Chinese world which had commanded their allegiance since they set out from their villages.

The value of the system for the merchant-creditors impressed an editorial writer of the *Alta California* in 1855. Wealthy Chinese traders, he observed, paid for the sojourners' transportation and took them "into the mines and derived the entire profit of their labor." These indentured emigrants were "in fact little better than slaves, and their own countrymen were their master." They "have laws of their own," the editor emphasized, "and they enforce their contracts not only without, but in defiance of our State laws."[8] In May, 1859, a reporter of the Stockton *Argus* described the arrival of Chinese miners at Stockton who were "bundled on board the boat like so many cattle." Their countrymen, engaged in mining operations, had traveled in the cabin and "brought them from China for the purpose of speculating in their labor."[9] One year later the Stockton *Republican* lamented that Chinese agents forwarded "load after load" of indentured emigrants "in the same manner as other freight."[10]

Western vessels had linked Kwangtung with California after the discovery of gold attracted the shipping fleets. Hastily unloaded at San Francisco, the craft were dispatched to China, where they "either competed successfully with English ships for return cargoes to the Atlantic, or were profitably employed" in carrying emigrants to California.[11] Chinese merchants, recently established in San Francisco and without lines of communication to Hongkong equal to those of the traditional junk routes in Southeast Asia, came to rely on western sailing vessels for transporting their countrymen. As charterers or owners of an ill-assorted fleet, these traders, with the aid of such San Francisco commission merchants as Cornelius Koopmanschap, controlled the flow of Chinese emigrants to California as effectively as to Malaysia.[12]

The transport of sojourners employed shipping at a time of great demand for freight. It relieved the depression in one aspect of an overexpanded trading economy. High freight rates made the traffic so lucrative that ships frequently did not wait for additional cargo, but took passengers aboard and sailed in ballast. Contemporary observers speculated about the profits of ship owners or charterers. Chinese merchant-creditors earned no quick return whether they owned or chartered ships to transport the emigrants whose passage they furnished. For a profitable return on their considerable investment they speculated not on the shipping venture but on the labor potential of their countrymen in California.[13] Western ship owners, on the other hand, reaped their money as soon as the Chinese paid for the vessels they chartered.

The fare, at the lowest estimate, amounted to forty dollars for the voyage to San Francisco and twenty dollars for the return trip. Most observers considered fifty dollars as average fee.[14] The easy profits attracted a multitude of vessels. Their owners represented most nations trading with China. American craft soon overcame the numerical superiority which British bottoms originally enjoyed. Size and type of the ships varied as larger boats came to dominate the shipping business and were utilized in the human traffic. In the 1840's, a sailing vessel of five hundred tons burden still represented a respectable ship; in the first quarter of the 1860's, nearly half the craft at Hongkong registered over a thousand tons.[15]

Isolated news items, merchant circulars, and Chinese notes furnish a composite picture of the passage.[16] With minor exceptions, Hongkong served as point of departure.[17] The chaotic state of the Pearl River Delta, foreign wars, internal unrest, and rebellion drove Western shipping into the British colony. Hongkong also freed sea captains and Chinese brokers from the clutches of avaricious officials at Whampoa or the barracoons of coolie traders at Macao. Proclaimed a free port in 1841, Hongkong required no duties, not even bills of health since, according to the bon mot of a United States consul, no new disease could be imported.[18]

The regulations of Western powers hardly affected Chinese emigration before the 1880's.[19] In the United States, inadequate legislation went hand in hand with a lack of information about the nature of the traffic. The regimentation, the squalor of the crowded quarters, and the "fearful mortality" among the passengers, from time to time directed the compassion of Americans to conditions that threw "the most indefatigable slaver which ever sailed on the African coast completely in the shade."[20] However, court actions failed to awaken the conscience of ship owners who counted upon the confiscation of worthless hulks as a matter of course and calculated their possible loss into the expenses of the ventures. The merchant community's credo of the destiny of American commerce in China and the clamor for the trade's undisturbed development, lent quasi-sanction to the traffic. Its oppressive elements were accepted as a matter of course, perhaps because they seemed to resemble the stern shipboard discipline which many Californians had experienced in the not-too-distant past. Incapable of recognizing the sojourners as human beings through the barrier of the Chinese world, San Franciscans came to view the traffic's seedier sides as symptomatic of Chinese emigration.[21]

While the credit-ticket system was the dominant mode of traveling from Hongkong to San Francisco, the passage was made at times under conditions similar to the thinly-veiled slave traffic of the coolie system. The credit-ticket system became partly a disguised slave trade, managed chiefly by Chinese crimps and compradors. Middlemen lured artisans, peasants, and laborers into barracoons and sold them to ticket agents. At the Chinese ports and at San Francisco, the sojourners were confined, watched, and terrorized by the thugs of Chinese societies who acted in the creditors' interest.[22]

The travelers, waiting for the day of departure, were induced to gamble and lost money. Additional costs were added to the passage fee. Skippers frequently charged the emigrants for fitting up bunks or water tanks in the steerage. Harry Parkes, the Chinese interpreter of the Superintendent of British Trade in China, noted that the merchant-creditors paid fifty dollars for the passage and twenty dollars as additional expenses of the emigrants, on "the condition of receiving" in return "the sum of two hundred dollars." Most of the travelers accepted any arrangement that promised their transportation to the Golden Hills without realizing their financial obligations. The prospect of returning to China with two or three hundred dollars was inducement enough for men whose total annual income at home rarely amounted to one-tenth that sum; no venture for such princely gain was deemed too arduous.[23]

The emigrants to California traveled in junks, lorchas, or sampans over the waterways of the Pearl River Delta from their villages to Hongkong.[24] Messages from Chinese in California circulating through the hamlets, reports of returned sojourners reminiscing on their success, broadsides and open letters for and against emigration, and the rumors about the distant riches radiating from the shipping centers of South China filled the imagination of the travelers.[25] In company with other sojourners, the emigrants cast off before daybreak to avoid an encounter with fellow villagers and the possibility of hearing unlucky words which might endanger their enterprise. A roll of bedding and a bamboo basket with netting on the top, containing shoes, hat, and provisions, represented their worldly possessions.[26] At Hongkong, passage brokers provided a bunk in a dormitory, or friends and relatives furnished a domicile until the day of departure arrived.

The emigrants' limited contact with the strange environment of a Western sailing vessel served as an indicator of their relationship with the barbarian world for their entire sojourn. The travelers lined up on deck for inspection. After a mate had counted noses and tickets, to see that the charterers kept the bargain, the emigrants descended to their quarters below. With the exception of the cooks, few came up on deck during the voyage. Several bills of lading suggest that there might not have been room on the upper deck.[27] But even when ships sailed with a clear deck, the steerage was the easiest place to control large numbers of emigrants. It was one of the surest ways to avoid fights between the Chinese and the crew.

The length and course of the voyage varied with the season.[28] Between 1848 and 1867, a vast number of Chinese emigrants lived for an average of two months at the mercy of the ocean, their bosses and comrades, and the ships' crews. Calm days presented their particular problems. While the ship drifted idly on the smooth sea, and the sailors amused themselves by fishing, the emigrants gambled in their quarters or lay in their bunks, vainly listening for the yells, creaks, and gongs of their junks. Such tension-filled days brought fights between sailors and travelers and quarrels among the Chinese. In addition, the quality of the provisions and the neglect of the quarters caused friction between the emigrants and their countrymen who represented contractors or charterers.

During the course of the voyage, the dark, dank depths of the sailing vessels grew increasingly oppressive to men who were there under compulsion and afflicted by superstition, apprehension, and dreams of their destination. When barrel after barrel of rotten pork had to be thrown overboard; when rough seas prevented the travelers from using the badly constructed cooking places, arranged with an eye to maximum economy on the crowded main deck; when cheaply-built bunks continued to break down to the risk of heads and limbs, the strain-charged air could explode at any moment. While the Chinese insisted on settling their disturbances in their own way, the sailors liked to put down unrest by force. In the event of a clash with the crew, the Chinese swarmed up from the lower decks, hurling pieces of lumber and brickbats from the cooking places. Forced to retreat, the emigrants usually smeared blood over the faces of their wounded comrades and left them on the upper deck as if dead. Such moments tested the ability of captain and officers to prevent an open battle.[29]

The average captain handled the difficult task capably. His name disappeared behind the stories of the few who bungled their job or earned the praise of their Chinese passengers. There were few disturbances on Chinese emigrant ships "in which the commanders have not been blameworthy in a very high degree," Dr. John Bowring, Superintendent of British Trade in China, commented.[30] On other occasions the travelers presented their skippers with rings and flags as expressions of their gratitude for a safe voyage and friendly treatment.[31] Only in these instances did the emigrants break through the invisible barrier of the Chinese world, which confined them, and appeared more as a group of human beings than mere figures in the ships' papers and the registers of harbor masters. Generally the complete isolation of the sojourners from the world of Western shipping was one of the characteristics of the traffic.

When the emigrants' eager eyes finally caught the first glimmer of the Golden Gate, they strained every sense to catch the golden hues with which their imagination had invested the gateway to California. However, nothing but rock formations crowned with fog gratified their gaze. The stream of Western travelers who approached San Francisco by sea in the 1840's and 1850's, sensed the raw, cold, and disagreeable scene. To the Chinese, however, the barren shoreline, as far as it was visible through the mist, much resembled the bleak islands of the Pearl River's estuary and presaged an equally familiar world of unrewarding work.

Noise and confusion accompanied the disembarkation on the wharves of San Francisco. Baskets, matting, hats, and bamboo poles covered the pier that was crowded with boatmen, agents of Chinese merchants, draymen, custom officials, and spectators. Suddenly, as a traveler remembered, "out of the general babble some one called out in our local dialect, and, like sheep recognizing the voice only, we blindly followed and soon were piling into one of the waiting wagons." Everything appeared so "strange and exciting," he confessed, that his memory of the landing was "just a big blur." The Chinese quarter was the destination of other groups who marched in single file through the streets, carrying their luggage suspended from the ends of bamboo poles slung across their shoulders. The first night in the strange country the newcomers slept in the dormitories owned by the companies under whose management they had made the long sea voyage, safely confined within the narrow limits of a Chinese world that had harbored them ever since they departed from their villages.[32]

The adaptation of the credit-ticket system to the passage between Hongkong and San Francisco extended the physical and social framework of the Chinese world to California. The maintenance of this world within the United States required further modifications to sustain the pattern of indenture without the aid of American courts and customs. The basic sentiments of Californians, derived from their experience with the Indians and with Negro slavery, and influenced by their exalted vision of the state's future, ran counter to an extension to California of the Chinese concept of debt bondage. Chinese merchants utilized district companies and kinship organizations as instruments of extra-legal control and secured the continuation of the pattern. The application of the traditional mode of Chinese emigration to the passage facilitated transplanting the system of oppression. Characterized in terms not of liberty but of survival, a Chinese California emerged, isolated from, yet part of, Western development.

Notes

1. William Speer and Augustus W. Loomis, missionaries of the Presbyterian Board of Foreign Missions to the Chinese in California, in their reports to the Secretary of the Presbyterian Board of Foreign Missions in New York between 1853 and 1865, frequently refer to this goal of the Chinese emigrants. *Correspondence of the Presbyterian Board of Foreign Missions*, Presbyterian Historical Society, Philadelphia. See also *Hsia-Erh Kuan-Chen* [Gathered Gems from Far and Near] (Hongkong), II (January 1, 1854), 5b–7b; "Letter from Fou Sin to his Father & Brothers," printed in a pamphlet, *Murder of M[artin] V. B. Griswold, By Five Chinese Assassins* . . . (Jackson, Calif., 1858), pp. 25–26.

2. E[lihu] Doty and W[illiam] J. Pohlman, "Journal of a Tour on the Island of Borneo [in the Districts of Sambas and Pontianak], November, 1838"; W[illiam] Youngblood and E[lbert] Nevius, "Journal [of Travels in Western Borneo in March, 1840]"; [Elbert Nevius and William Youngblood], "Journal of a Tour to Mandoor and Sandak [April, 1840]," *Papers of the American Board of Commissioners for Foreign Missions, Borneo Mission, 1838–1844,* I–II, Houghton Library, Harvard University; John Crawford, *History of the Indian Archipelago* ... (3 vols., Edinburgh, 1820), I, 135, III, 183; Charles Gutzlaff, *Journal of Three Voyages Along the Coast of China, in 1831, 1832 & 1833* ... (London, 1834), pp. 165–168; [Siah U Chin], "Remittances by Chinese Immigrants in Singapore to Their Families in China," *Journal of the Indian Archipelago and Eastern Asia* (Singapore), I ([January–February], 1847), 35–37; C[oenrad] J. Temminck, *Coup-D'Oeil Général sur Les Possessions Néerlandaises dans L'Inde Archipélagique* (3 vols., Leiden, 1847), II, 169; Siah U Chin, "The Chinese in Singapore; General Sketch of the Numbers, Tribes, and Avocations of the Chinese in Singapore," *Journal of the Indian Archipelago and Eastern Asia* II ([May], 1848), 285–287; G. F. Davidson, *Trade and Travel in the Far East; or Recollections of the Twenty-one Years Passed in Java, Singapore, Australia, and China* (London, 1848), p. 46; [Johan Hendrick Croockewitcz], "De Tinmijnen van Malaka," *Tijdschrift voor Nederlandsch Indie* (Zaltbommel, Netherlands), XIII (November, 1851), 301–302; "Notes on the Chinese of Pinang," *Journal of the Indian Archipelago and Eastern Asia,* VIII ([January–February], 1854), 2–3.

3. Persia Crawford Campbell, *Chinese Coolie Emigration to Countries within the British Empire* (London, 1923); Watt Stewart, *Chinese Bondage in Peru, 1849–1874* (Durham, North Carolina, 1951).

4. For an example, see William Speer, *China and California; Their Relations, Past and Present. A Lecture in Conclusion of a Series in Relation to the Chinese People, Delivered in the Stockton Street Presbyterian Church, San Francisco, June 28, 1853* (San Francisco, 1853), pp. 13–16; "What are Coolies?" San Francisco *Oriental, or Tung-Ngai San-Luk,* January 11, 1855; *An Humble Plea addressed to the Legislature of California, In Behalf of the Immigrants from the Empire of China to this State* (San Francisco, 1856); "Democracy of the Chinese," *Harper's New Monthly Magazine,* XXXVII (November, 1868), 839–848; *The Oldest and the Newest Empire: China and the United States* (Hartford, Conn., 1870), pp. 462–492; San Francisco *Alta California,* April 2, 1857; San Francisco *Herald,* July 14, 1853; December 8, 1855.

5. San Francisco *Alta California,* March 8, 1852.

6. *Ibid.,* March 23, 1851; San Francisco *Herald,* March 25, 1851.

7. Speer to Walter Lowrie, December 18, 1852; Loomis to Lowrie, March 1, 9; June 25, September 19, 1860; April 17, 1862; June 29, 1863; March 5, 1864; *Correspondence of the Presbyterian Board for Foreign Missions;* San Francisco *Alta California,* September 20, October 1, 1849; May 11, 1850; March 31, 1851; March 1, August 28, October 1, 18, 1852; March 24, 28, April 25, May 20, September 28, 1853; February 2, March 25, 1854; August 26, September 16, 1856; October 15, 1857; May 30, July 17, 23, August 13, 1858; June 16, October 29, November 2, 3, December 13, 1859; February 9, 26, May 24, July 7, October 20, 1860; January 14, 28, March 1, 5, 16, 17, 19, April 16, August 22, 1861; March 12, May 7, October 17, November 14, 1862; May 5, July 28, December 9, 1864; March 2, 14, June 6, 1865; January 14, April 1, 5, July 26, September 16, 1866; May 12, June 9, September 29, 1867; May 9, 1868; June 24, 1869;

San Francisco *Herald*, April 12, August 29, 1852; May 16, 23, 1853; January 11, 1854; October 27, 1855; July 2, 18, 24, August 13, 1858; July 6, 1859; May 12, June 16, 1860.

8. San Francisco *Alta California*, February 21, 1855.

9. *Ibid.*, quoting Stockton *Argus*, May 16, 21, 1859.

10. *Ibid.*, quoting Stockton *Republican*, September 2, December 5, 1860. For additional descriptions see San Francisco *Alta California*, June 12, November 26, 1861; May 8, 24, 1862; January 15, July 6, 1863; April 26, 27, July 11, 1864; July 26, August 14, 15, 16, 18, 23, 1866; May 27, June 30, September 2, 1867; July 15, 1869; San Francisco *Herald*, May 20, 1852; May 29, August 4, 1853; February 14, August 22, 1854; February 4, 1855; April 20, 1858; May 20, 1859; July 23, 1861; San Francisco *California Police Gazette*, May 25, June 8, 1867; May 29, 1869; Sacramento *Placer Times*, March 2, 1850.

11. Frank Soulé, John H. Gihon, and James Nisbet, *The Annals of San Francisco* ... (New York, 1855), p. 419.

12. San Francisco *Alta California*, June 3, September 18, 19, October 30, 1853; June 27, 29, July 1, August 22, 1854; San Francisco *Herald*, September 17, 1853; October 18, 1855. For the leading position among Western firms which Cornelius Koopmanschap gained in the traffic of Chinese emigrants during the 1860's see San Francisco *Alta California*, January 15, 1863; July 15, 30, 1869; New York *World*, July 20, 21, 1869; New York *Evening Post*, July 15, 20, 1869; New Orleans *Daily Picayune*, July 14, 15, 28, August 6, October 2, 4, 14, 1869; January 6, 8, 9, 1870; St. Louis *Republican*, July 15, 1869 (*Bancroft Scraps, Chinese Clippings*, VI, 144–148, Bancroft Library, University of California); "The Chinese Again," *Hunt's Merchants' Magazine*, LXI (September 1869), 214; *U.S. Senate Report 689*, 44 Cong., 2 Sess., p. 76.

13. San Francisco *Herald*, August 17, 1852; May 9, 1854; May 7, 1856; San Francisco *Alta California*, May 16, June 27, August 22, 1854; San Francisco *Daily Evening News and Evening Picayune*, January 28, 1854. The circulars of the house of King & Co. at Canton and the firm of Rawle, Brinker & Co. at Hongkong readily documented the possibility of the traffic with detailed lists of the ships carrying Chinese passengers. San Francisco *Herald*, June 12, August 17, 1852. Eldon Griffin, *Clippers and Consuls; American Consular and Commercial Relations with Eastern Asia, 1845–1860* (Ann Arbor, Mich., 1938), reviewed in detail the American commerce with China during the period.

14. Peter Parker to Daniel Webster, March 27, 1852. *U.S. Senate Ex. Doc. 99*, 34 Cong., 1 Sess., pp. 119–120; San Francisco *Alta California*, April 25, 1852; San Francisco *Herald*, February 11, 14, 1856; Speer, *Humble Plea*, p. 7; E[rnest] J. Eitel, *Europe in China; The History of Hongkong from the Beginning to the Year 1882* (London, 1882), p. 259.

15. San Francisco *Herald*, March 13, August 17, 1852; March 29, 1853; Hongkong *China Mail*, April 3, 1860.

16. The mode of coming received no attention in the secondary accounts discussing the Chinese in the United States. Russell H. Conwell, *Why and How. Why the Chinese Emigrate, and the Means They Adopt for the Purpose of Reaching America. With Sketches of Travels, Amusing Incidents, Social Customs, &c.* (Boston, 1871), pp. 212–213, formed the exception and gave a sketch of Chinese life on one of "those palace steamships owned by the Pacific Mail Steamship Company."

17. San Francisco *Herald*, June 7, 1853; San Francisco *Alta California*, January 3, 1857; January 3, 1860.

18. *U.S. Senate Ex. Doc. 107*, 4 vols., 34 Cong., 1 Sess., III, 638; Hosea Ballou Morse, *The International Relations of the Chinese Empire* (3 vols., New York, 1910–18), I, 292.

19. San Francisco *Herald*, September 9, 1854, quoting *China Mail;* Harley F. McNair, *The Chinese Abroad, Their Position and Protection; A Study in International Law and Relations* (Shanghai, 1926), pp. 1–27, gives details of the legal aspects of Chinese emigration.

20. San Francisco *Herald*, August 12, 1854.

21. *Ibid.*, October 27, December 29, 1851; February 18, March 22, July 23, November 1, 1853; July 20, 21, 22, 23, 24, 25, 26, 27, August 8, 12, 13, 15, 17, 19, 21, 22, 24, 26, 27, September 4, 16, 22, 23, 28, 30, October 9, December 29, 1854; December 18, 1855; March 16, May 7, 1856; January 28, 1857; April 20, 1858; San Francisco *Alta California*, June 29, October 19, 1852; July 19, 21, 22, 27, 28, 29, August 1, 4, 12, 15, 17, 18, 19, 24, 26, September 1, 11, 20, 21, 22, 23, 24, 27, 28, October 7, 8, 1854; September 10, 13, 1855; May 22, July 11, 1857; February 19, 1858; February 20, March 1, 5, 1862; August 3, 16, September 18, 1866; July 15, 1869; San Francisco *Occidental and Vanguard*, July 5, 1867.

22. Speer to Lowrie, November 15, December 16, 1852; Loomis to Lowrie, November 18, 1859; March 1, June 25, 1860; April 17, 1862; June 29, 1863; *Correspondence of the Presbyterian Board for Foreign Missions;* San Francisco *Oriental*, January 11, April 28, May 26, 1855; San Francisco *Alta California*, July 8, August 11, 1851; June 16, October 1, 3, 1852; January 14, 16, 21, May 31, June 7, November 17, 18, 1853; August 22, October 14, 1854; April 5, 1856; June 19, 1859; January 24, August 16, 1860; August 23, 1864; August 17, 1867, and quoting Sonora *Union Democrat*, December 10, 1856; San Francisco *Herald*, July 28, October 9, 1851; June 9, 1852; January 13, May 28, 29, 1853; August 27, September 24, 1854; January 10, 1857; "Chinese Mercantile Operations [in San Francisco]," *Hunt's Merchants' Magazine*, XXXI (September, 1854), 391; Rev. J. C. Holbrook, "Chinadom in California. In Two Papers—Paper the First," *Hutchings' Illustrated California Magazine*, IV (September, 1859), 130; Frank Marryat, *Mountains and Molehills; or Recollections of a Burnt Journal* (New York, 1855), pp. 172, 299–300; Speer, *Oldest and Newest Empire*, pp. 554–557; Hemman Hoffmann, *Californien, Nevada und Mexico. Wanderungen* [March, 1864–June, 1867] *eines Polytechnikers* (Basel, 1879), p. 49; J[ames] O'Meara, "The Chinese in Early Days," *Overland Monthly*, III (2nd ser., May 1884), 480.

23. Harry Parkes, "General Remarks on Chinese Emigration," *British Parliamentary Papers, 1852–53*, LXVIII [263], 26.

24. Yan Pou Lee, *When I Was A Boy in China* (Boston, [1887]), pp. 96–97.

25. Russell & Co. to William Appleton, April 22, 1849; June 19, 1850, *Dexter MSS;* Appleton to George D. Carter, February 5, 1849, *Appleton MSS,* Baker Library, Harvard University; *U.S. House of Rep. Ex. Doc. 123*, 33 Cong., 1 Sess., pp. 83–85; *U.S. Senate Ex. Doc. 99*, 34 Cong., 1 Sess., pp. 102–103, 178–179; Adam W. Elmslie [British Consul at Canton] to Dr. John Bowring, August 25, 1852, *British Parliamentary Papers, 1852–53*, LXVIII [263], 7–8; "Journal of Occurrences: . . . emigration of Chinese to America . . ," *Chinese Repository* (Can-

ton), XIX (September, 1850), 510–511; San Francisco Alta California, February 17, March 29, June 12, 1852; September 8, 1856.

26. Kin Huie, Reminiscences (Peking, 1932), p. 12.

27. San Francisco Alta California, June 10, 14, 1850; June 29, 1852; San Francisco Herald, June 30, 1852; March 29, 1853.

28. For the shortest and the longest voyages of Chinese immigrants between Hong-kong and San Francisco, see San Francisco Herald, April 29, 30, 1853; San Francisco Alta, September 11, 1854; January 3, 1857. For the course turn to Thomas G. Cary, "Chinese in California—Clipper Ships," MS, Houghton Library, Harvard University, p. 14; San Francisco Alta, April 9, 1858; February 25, 1865; M[atthew] F. Maury, Explanations and Sailing Instructions to Accompany the Wind and Current Charts (Washington, D.C., 1851), p. 309; [Pacific Mail Steamship Co.], A Sketch of the Route to California, China and Japan, via the Isthmus of Panama (San Francisco, 1867), p. 95.

29. China Mail, April 29, 1852; October 14, 1854; July 2, 1857; August 23, 1864. Andrew Wilson, in the latter 1850's editor of the Hongkong China Mail, described his experiences with Chinese emigrants on a trip to California in a letter published in the China Mail, July 11, 1861. See also John Haskell Kemble (ed.), "Andrew Wilson's 'Jottings' on Civil War California," California Historical Society Quarterly, XXXII (September, 1953), 213–214.

30. Dr. John Bowring to the Earl of Malmesbury, May 17, 1852, British Parliamentary Papers, 1852–53, LXVIII [263], 2. For the disaster on the American ship Robert Bowne, to which Dr. Bowring referred, see U.S. Senate Ex. Doc. 99, 34 Cong., 1 Sess., pp. 119–165; Hongkong Friend of China, April 28, 1852; China Mail, April 29, 1852; Hongkong Overland Register, May 18, 1852; San Francisco Herald, June 28, 30, July 1, 20, August 15, October 19, 1852; San Francisco Alta California, June 29, July 20, 1852; Earl Swisher (ed.), China's Management of the American Barbarians; A Study of Sino-American Relations, 1841–1861, with Documents (New Haven, Conn., [1953]), pp. 199–203.

31. San Francisco Alta California, June 12, 1852; August 1, 1854; February 26, 1856; July 4, 1857; May 21, 1860; San Francisco Herald, July 4, 1854.

32. Loomis to Walter Lowrie, March 1, 1860, Correspondence of the Presbyterian Board of Foreign Missions; San Francisco Alta California, April 27, July 24, August 20, 22, 1851; February 26, March 14, 28, June 12, September 25, 1852; April 20, October 14, 1854; May 6, 1857; August 3, 1860; October 17, 1861; San Francisco Herald, May 17, June 26, August 20, 1851; April 11, 12, June 27, 1852; March 2, November 1, 1853; July 2, 6, 1857; San Francisco Daily Evening News and Evening Picayune, February 16, 1854; Huie, Reminiscences, p. 24.

Selected Bibliography

A. General Works

Allport, Gordon W. *The Nature of Prejudice*. New York: Anchor, 1954.

Bennett, Lerone. *Before the Mayflower*. New York: Penguin, 1962.

Burma, John H., ed. *Mexican-Americans in the United States*. Cambridge, Mass.: Schenkman, 1970.

Farb, Peter. *Man's Rise to Civilization, As Shown by the Indians of North America From the Primeval Times to the Coming of the Industrial State*. New York: Avon, 1968.

Franklin, John Hope. *From Slavery to Freedom*. New York: Vintage, 1967.

Glazer, Nathan and Daniel Patrick Moynihan. *Beyond the Melting Pot: The Negroes, Puerto Ricans, Jews, Italians, and Irish of New York City*. Cambridge: M.I.T. Press, 1963.

Gordon, Milton M. *Assimilation in American Life*. New York: Oxford University Press, 1964.

Gossett, Thomas F. *Race: The History of an Idea in America*. New York: Schocken, 1963.

Grebler, Leo, Joan W. Moore, and Ralph C. Guzman. *The Mexican-American People: The Nation's Second Largest Minority*. New York: Free Press, 1970.

Hagan, William T. *American Indians*. Chicago: University of Chicago Press, 1961.

Handlin, Oscar. *Race and Nationality in American Life*. New York: Anchor, 1957.

Kitano, Harry H. *The Japanese-Americans: The Evolution of a Subculture*. New York: Prentice-Hall, 1969.

Kovel, Joel. *White Racism: A Psychohistory*. New York: Vintage, 1970.

Lee, Rose Hum. *The Chinese in the United States of America*. Hong Kong: Hong Kong University Press, 1960.

McWilliams, Carey. *North From Mexico: The Spanish-Speaking People of the United States*. Westport, Conn.: Greenwood, 1948.

Meier, August and Elliott M. Rudwick. *From Plantation to Ghetto*. New York: Hill and Wang, 1966.

Myers, Gustavus. *History of Bigotry in the United States*. New York: Capricorn, 1943.

Nash, Gary B. and Richard Weiss, eds. *The Great Fear: Race in the Mind of America*. New York: Holt, 1970.

Schwartz, Barry M. and Robert Disch. *White Racism: Its History, Pathology, and Practice*. New York: Dell, 1970.

Spicer, Edward H. *A Short History of the Indians of the United States*. New York: Anvil, 1969.

B. The Seventeenth and Eighteenth Centuries

Blacks

Greene, Lorenzo. *The Negro in Colonial New England*. New York: Atheneum, 1942.

Jordan, Winthrop. *White Over Black: American Attitudes Toward the Negro, 1550–1812*. New York: Penguin, 1968.

Klingberg, Frank. *An Appraisal of the Negro in Colonial South Carolina*. Toronto: Associated Publishers, 1941.

Mannix, Daniel, and Malcolm Cowley. *Black Cargoes: A History of the Atlantic Slave Trade*. New York: Viking, 1962.

Mellon, Matthew T. *Early American Views on Negro Slavery*. New York: Mentor, 1934, 1969.

Quarles, Benjamin. *The Negro in the American Revolution*. Chapel Hill: University of North Carolina Press, 1961.

Robinson, Donald. *Slavery in the Structure of American Politics, 1765–1820*. New York: Harcourt, 1971.

Tate, Thad W. *The Negro in Eighteenth-Century Williamsburg*. Charlottesville: University of Virginia Press, 1966.

Zilversmit, Arthur. *The First Emancipation: The Abolition of Slavery in the North*. Chicago: University of Chicago Press, 1967.

Indians

Lauber, Almon W. *Indian Slavery in Colonial Times Within the Present Limits of the United States*. New York: Columbia University Press, 1913.

Leach, Douglas E. *Flintlock and Tomahawk: New England in King Philip's War*. New York: Norton, 1958.

Milling, Chapman J. *Red Carolinians*. Chapel Hill: University of North Carolina Press, 1940.

Trelease, Allen W. *Indian Affairs in Colonial New York: Seventeenth Century*. Ithaca, N. Y.: Cornell University Press, 1960.

Vaughan, Alden T. *The New England Frontier: Puritans and Indians, 1620–1675.* Boston: Little, Brown, 1965.

Wallace, Anthony F. C. *King of the Delawares: Teedyuscung.* Philadelphia: University of Pennsylvania Press, 1949.

C. The Nineteenth Century

Blacks

Aptheker, Herbert. *American Negro Slave Revolts.* New York: International Publishers, 1943.

Carroll, Joseph C. *Slave Insurrections in the United States.* Westport, Conn.: Negro Universities Press, 1938.

DuBois, W. E. B. *Black Reconstruction in America.* Cleveland: Meridian, 1935.

Elkins, Stanley. *Slavery: A Problem in American Institutional and Intellectual Life.* Chicago: University of Chicago Press, 1959.

Genovese, Eugene. *The Political Economy of Slavery.* New York: Vintage, 1961.

Litwack, Leon F. *North of Slavery: The Negro in the Free States, 1790–1860.* Chicago: University of Chicago Press, 1961.

Logan, Rayford W. *The Betrayal of the Negro: From Rutherford B. Hayes to Woodrow Wilson.* New York: Collier, 1965.

McPherson, James. *The Negro's Civil War.* New York: Vintage, 1965.

Meier, August. *Negro Thought in America, 1880–1915.* Ann Arbor: University of Michigan Press, 1963.

Quarles, Benjamin. *Black Abolitionists.* New York: Oxford University Press, 1969.

Stampp, Kenneth. *The Peculiar Institution.* New York: Vintage, 1956.

Starobin, Robert S. *Industrial Slavery in the Old South.* New York: Oxford University Press, 1970.

Wade, Richard. *Slavery in the Cities.* New York: Oxford University Press, 1964.

Wood, Forrest G. *Black Scare: The Racist Response to Emancipation and Reconstruction.* Berkeley: University of California Press, 1968.

Woodward, C. Vann. *The Strange Career of Jim Crow.* New York: Oxford University Press, 1955.

Indians

Abel, Annie. *The Slaveholding Indians,* 3 vols. Glendale, Calif.: Arthur H. Clark, 1915–1925.

Andrist, Ralph K. *The Long Death: The Last Days of the Plains Indians.* New York: Collier, 1964.

Brown, Dee. *Bury My Heart at Wounded Knee.* New York: Holt, 1970.

DeRosier, Arthur Jr. *The Removal of the Choctaw Indians.* Knoxville: University of Tennessee Press, 1970.

Downes, Randolph C. *Council Fires On the Upper Ohio.* Pittsburgh: University of Pittsburgh Press, 1940.

Ewers, John C. *The Blackfeet: Raiders on the Northwestern Plains.* Norman: University of Oklahoma Press, 1958.

Foreman, Grant. *Indian Removal: The Emigration of the Five Civilized Tribes of Indians.* Norman: University of Oklahoma Press, 1953.

Fritz, Henry E. *The Movement for Indian Assimilation, 1860–1890.* Philadelphia: University of Pennsylvania Press, 1963.

Hagan, William T. *The Sac and Fox Indians.* Norman: University of Oklahoma Press, 1958.

Horsman, Reginald. *Expansion and American Indian Policy, 1783–1812.* East Lansing: Michigan State University Press, 1967.

Priest, Loring B. *Uncle Sam's Stepchildren: The Reformation of United States Indian Policy, 1865–1887.* New Brunswick: Rutgers University Press, 1942.

Prucha, Francis P. *American Indian Policy in the Formative Years, 1790–1834.* Lincoln: University of Nebraska Press, 1962.

Tucker, Glenn. *Tecumseh.* Indianapolis: Bobbs-Merrill, 1956.

Wallace, Ernest and E. Adamson Hoebel. *The Comanches: Lords of the South Plains.* Norman: University of Oklahoma Press, 1953.

Mexican-Americans

Burns, Walter Noble. *The Robin Hood of El Dorado: The Saga of Joaquin Murietta.* New York: Coward-McCann, 1932.

Greenwood, Robert. *The California Outlaw: Tiburcio Vasquez.* Georgetown, Calif.: Talisman Press, 1960.

Pitt, Leonard. *The Decline of the Californios: A Social History of the Spanish-Speaking Californians, 1846–1890.* Berkeley: University of California Press, 1966.

Chinese-Americans

Barth, Gunther. *Bitter Strength: A History of the Chinese in the United States, 1850–1870.* Cambridge: Harvard University Press, 1964.

Chiu, Ping. *Chinese Labor in California, 1850–1880.* Madison: Historical Society of Wisconsin, 1963.

Coolidge, Mary. *Chinese Immigration.* New York: Henry Holt, 1909.

Miller, Stuart C. *The Unwelcome Immigrant: The American Image of the Chinese, 1785–1882.* Berkeley: University of California Press, 1969.

Sandmeyer, Elmer C. *The Anti-Chinese Movement in California.* Urbana: University of Illinois Press, 1939.

D. The Twentieth Century

Blacks

Cleaver, Eldridge. *Soul On Ice.* New York: McGraw-Hill, 1968.

Cronon, E. David. *Black Moses: The Story of Marcus Garvey.* Madison: University of Wisconsin Press, 1955.

Jackson, Kenneth T. *The Ku Klux Klan in the City, 1915–1930*. New York: Oxford University Press, 1967.

Kellogg, Charles F. *NAACP: A History of the National Association for the Advancement of Colored People*, vol. 1. Baltimore: Johns Hopkins Press, 1967.

Lester, Julius. *Look Out Whitey: Black Power's Gon' Get Your Mama*. New York: Grove, 1968.

Lomax, Louis. *The Negro Revolt*. New York: Signet, 1962.

Malcolm X. *Autobiography of Malcolm X*. New York: Grove, 1964.

Osofsky, Gilbert. *Harlem: The Making of a Ghetto, 1890–1920*. New York: Torchbook, 1966.

Spear, Allan. *Black Chicago: The Making of a Negro Ghetto, 1890–1920*. Chicago: University of Chicago Press, 1967.

White, Walter. *Rope and Faggot: A Biography of Judge Lynch*. New York: Arno, 1928.

Indians

Deloria, Vine, Jr. *Custer Died for Your Sins: An Indian Manifesto*. New York: Macmillan, 1969.

Embry, Carlos B. *America's Concentration Camps*. New York: David McKay, 1956.

Kahn, Edgar, ed. *Our Brother's Keeper: The Indian in White America*. Cleveland: World Publishing, 1969.

Levine, Stuart and Nancy O. Lurie, eds. *The American Indian Today*. Deland, Fla.: Everett-Edwards, 1968.

Steiner, Stan. *The New Indians*. New York: Dell, 1968.

Mexican-Americans

Dunne, John Gregory. *Delano: The Story of the California Grape Strike*. New York: Farrar, Straus, 1967.

Heller, Celia S. *Mexican-American Youth: Forgotten Youth At the Crossroads*. New York: Random, 1966.

Kibbe, Pauline R. *Latin Americans in Texas*. Albuquerque: University of New Mexico Press, 1946.

Matthiesen, Peter. *Sal Si Puedes: Cesar Chavez and the New American Revolution*. New York: Random, 1969.

Nabokov, Peter. *Tijerina and the Courthouse Raid*. Albuquerque: University of New Mexico Press, 1969.

Peattie, Lisa Redfield. *The View From the Barrio*. Ann Arbor: University of Michigan Press, 1968.

Tuck, Ruth D. *Not With the Fist: Mexican-Americans in a Southwest City*. New York: Harcourt, 1946.

Japanese-Americans

Daniels, Roger. *The Politics of Prejudice: The Anti-Japanese Movement in California and the Struggle for Japanese Exclusion.* New York: Atheneum, 1962.

Grodzins, Morton. *Americans Betrayed: Politics and the Japanese Evacuation.* Chicago: University of Chicago Press, 1949.

Hosokawa, Bill. *Nisei: The Quiet Americans.* New York: Morrow, 1969.

Rademaker, John. *These Are Americans: The Japanese-Americans in Hawaii in World War II.* Palo Alto, Calif.: Pacific Books, 1951.

Puerto Ricans

Chenault, Lawrence R. *The Puerto Rican Migrant in New York City.* New York: Russell and Russell, 1938.

Lewis, Oscar. *La Vida: A Puerto Rican Family in the Culture of Poverty—San Juan and New York.* New York: Random, 1966.

Senior, Clarence. *The Puerto Ricans: Strangers—Then Neighbors.* Chicago: Quadrangle, 1961.

Sexton, Patricia Cayo. *Spanish Harlem.* New York: Harper and Row, 1965.

Wakefield, Dan. *Island in the City.* New York: Corinth Books, 1959.

Filipinos

Bulosan, Carlos. *America is in the Heart.* New York: Harcourt, 1946.

Lasker, Bruno. *Filipino Immigration to Continental United States and to Hawaii.* Chicago: University of Chicago Press, 1931.

Index

Index

Index

Printed in U.S.A.